THE
# What Investment
GUIDE TO
# PERSONAL
# FINANCE

# THE
# What Investment
## GUIDE TO
# PERSONAL
# FINANCE

Rushmere Wynne
England

First published 1996
This edition (2nd impression) 1997

© Rushmere Wynne Limited 1996

British Library Cataloguing in Publication Data. A catalogue record for this book is
available from the British Library.

ISBN 0 948035 42 0

Designed and typeset by:
Michael Firth

Published by:
Rushmere Wynne Limited,
4-5 Harmill, Grovebury Road,
Leighton Buzzard, Bedfordshire LU7 8FF
Tel: 01525 853726
Fax: 01525 852037

Printed by:
Redwood Books Limited
Kennet House, Kennet Way
Trowbridge, Wiltshire BA14 8RN

# What Investment and Rushmere Wynne

This *What Investment Guide to Personal Finance* has been written to enable you to produce a comprehensive financial plan matched to your specific circumstances.

*What Investment* magazine has linked up with leading specialist financial publisher Rushmere Wynne to bring you a series of titles specially commisioned for *What Investment* readers.

These books form part of the *What Investment* book club. If you would like a brochure please telephone 01525 853726, or fax 01525 852037. If you prefer you can write to Rushmere Wynne, 4-5 Harmill, Grovebury Road, Leighton Buzzard, Beds LU7 8FF.

# HOW TO GET THE MAXIMUM BENEFIT
# FROM THIS BOOK

This book is divided into three sections. The first is about your life. Each chapter deals with a different lifestyle and gives a set of guides to keep you financially healthy. Not every idea or recommendation will apply to everyone falling into a particular lifestyle group. The aim is to set out the bones of the financial planning you need to do and leave you to add the details as and when you need or can afford to.

Also, remember that because each section looks at a different stage in your life, certain aspects may be covered in a different chapter. If, for example, you are buying a car and it is not covered in the chapter you are reading, then either have a flick through the preceding ones until you find it, or go to *Section Two* and find the CAR INSURANCE GUIDE there. All the guides mentioned in each chapter are listed at the end.

*Section Two* looks at the financial products themselves. Each guide explains what, for example, the investment trust is, that was mentioned in your lifestyle section, how it works and where you should get it from. Each explanation, where applicable, carries a warning about the possible pitfalls for you to be aware of.

*Section Three* allows you to do your own personal wealth check. Unless you know how much you earn and spend then you cannot begin to think about sorting out your finances. The wealth check sets out all the different categories where you may spend or which earn you money and then lets you decide how much you have left to play around with. The asset planner allows you to work out how much you are worth overall. This takes into account all the big things you own, such as your car and house, against what you owe such as the mortgage, and comes out with a total assets (or liabilities) figure. It can be used for inheritance tax planning for example, or when you are writing a will.

If you find, after filling in the wealth check, that the amount left over does not match what is actually in your bank account at the end of each month, it could provide a wonderful opportunity for you to track your finances for a while and see if there are areas of unnecessary spending which can be pruned back to give you more money to save or spend on something more important.

By reading this book thoroughly you should be well placed to enjoy a sound financial future.

## Good luck!

# CONTENTS

## SECTION 1: Lifestyles

## SECTION 2: Financial Guides

# SECTION 3:  Wealth Check

# INTRODUCTION

Financial planning is something that concerns all of us, yet it is a subject that many people pay scant attention to. No matter how large or small your investment portfolio may be, this is merely the icing on the cake. Investment strategy can only be properly considered once day-to-day financial planning has been dealt with.

This is why the first of our series of *What Investment Guides* deals with the general topic of Personal Finance. In the course of the Guide, we will tackle the full range of financial planning decision, from getting various forms of bank account and insurance cover, through consumer credit facilities to the more sophisticated forms of investment planning.

The most important aspect of taking control of your personal finances is to plan ahead properly. And planning ahead is what this guide is designed to help you to do. The first section gives a broad overview of the sorts of financial decision that you are likely to be faced with at various stages in your life, and points you in the direction of the relevant special chapters later in the book. The second section deals more specifically with particular financial subjects, including where to get professional advice. Then, in Section 3, we provide you with a 'Budget Planner', which gives you a practical framework for tackling the basic elements of your financial planning.

It is, of course, impossible to give specific advice for every set of individual circumstances, but the *What Investment Guide to Personal Finance* will show you where to start in most circumstances. Your financial planning needs will largely be determined by where you are in life – single or couple, with or without dependent children, working or retired – and by the resources you have at your disposal. Life assurance is likely to be a bigger priority if you have a young family than if you are single with no dependants, for example. But it is also important to be clear about your own financial goals. This is particularly true with regard to long-term investment plans, where the amount of time you intend to maintain your investments and the purpose to which they are going to be put should have an important bearing on the type of investments you choose. But the same logic should also apply throughout your financial planning.

Most of us will not have the resources to do everything we want, so it is important to set realistic priorities, and that requires careful thought.

It goes without saying that the earlier you start your financial planning, the more effective it is likely to be, but there is something in this guide for everyone, whatever your time of life. The *What Investment Guide to Personal Finance* provides a solid foundation for your general financial planning, a foundation on which readers can build a successful investment strategy.

*Keiron Root*
**Editor**
*What Investment*

# SECTION 1:
# Lifestyles

# CHAPTER ONE

# TEENAGERS

FINANCIAL life really starts at 16 when most people get their first part-time – or full-time – job. We move from being reliant on our parents for pocket money to earning our own money and the financial freedom that brings with it.

It is in our teens that we learn about the staples that make up our financial diet – the basics that will apply throughout our life. Forget the bread, pasta and potatoes – the financial staples are earning, saving and spending.

Most people take out their first bank account between the ages of 11 and 20, and even this seemingly simple step can be fraught with difficulty.

We all have different needs from our bank accounts, and these vary with age and earnings. Recognising this, the banks offer a vast array of accounts which, like pasta for example, come in every colour, shape and size.

Students, it has to be said, get the best deals from the banks and building societies. Working on the premise that if you get someone young enough he or she will stick with you for life, a whole array of goodies, ranging from cinema tickets and record vouchers to cash, are on offer for young savers. They also get a free overdraft cushion up to £1,000 in some cases – much higher than those who work can get.

Bank and building society accounts can be roughly divided into two categories – current accounts and savings accounts. When you are choosing a *current account* go for the maximum flexibility possible. If you slip into the red for a day or two at the end of the month or after a big purchase, how much is the bank going to charge you, both in interest and in fees? What about cheque books and cheque guarantee cards, linked credit cards and the ease of setting up direct debits and standing orders?

Also look at the accessibility of the bank or building society you choose. How near is the cash point? Do its hours of opening coincide with your lifestyle? Many of the banks now offer a 24-hour telephone banking service – is this right for you, or do you prefer to deal face to face with people?

*Savings accounts* are a different kettle of fish. Most people are looking for the highest return possible from the amount of money they have to save. Savings accounts operate by increasing the amount of interest they pay as your balance increases. So if you only have £100 to save, for example, the rate might be 0.5% whereas those with £10,000 will receive 5%.

Also the longer you are willing to tie your money up, the higher the interest will be. Remember though that if you take out a notice account – one where you must give the bank or building society a certain amount of notice, normally 30, 60 or 90 days – you will be penalised, through loss of interest, if you want to withdraw the money quicker. All interest is taxed at source, so if you don't have to pay tax tell your bank or building society and fill out the relevant Inland Revenue form (R85). See the BANK GUIDE and BUILDING SOCIETY GUIDE for further details.

Seventeen is the age of the car for most of us. Finally freedom hits us – we can go where we want, when we want, without having to rely on public transport, parents, siblings or friends to take us there.

Car insurance is compulsory in this country and the CAR GUIDE tells you all about getting car insurance, and the different forms. Always shop around before you buy insurance, be it for your car, life or home contents. There are lots of independent intermediaries who will look at the whole marketplace and find the best deal for you. The ADVISERS GUIDE tells you all about the different ways to get advice about investments and insurances and the differences between those offering you help.

The scenario laid out above will not fit everyone's lifestyle. Many people will leave school at the age of 16 (or 18) and be unable to get a job, in which case your local Department of Social Security office will be able to tell you what benefits you are entitled to. If you have children early then it is worth looking at Chapter 4, as this details what help is available as well as things to do if you have any spare cash.

Reaching 18 is the true coming of age in financial terms. We become financially 'legal' and can own shares and other investments in our own right. It can also be a time for decision making – do we stay on in education and go to university or go out and get a job?

With grants being cut it is getting more and more difficult to make ends meet. To make up the difference between what it will give and the actual cost of going to university the Government has set up the student loan scheme in addition to what the banks will lend.

However careful you are, it is unlikely that you will manage to leave university without some level of debt – the average is £3,000 – but this can be reduced by some careful budgeting and forward thinking.

Try turning to Section 3 and working through the wealth check. This will show you exactly how much money you have and how much you spend. Once it is laid out in black and white in front of you it is easier to identify your priorities and see the areas where you could cut back on spending.

For most people, going to university also entails moving away from home for the first time. Unless you went to boarding school it will be the first time that mum or dad is not there to cook your dinner at the end of the day. While a daunting prospect, living away from home is great fun – with no one to tell you what to eat or wear or what time to come in.

But it could all end in tears if you are not careful. The RENT GUIDE tells you all about the cost of moving out, from the deposit to ongoing costs such as gas bills to insuring your possessions. The HOME INSURANCE GUIDE explains about insuring your belongings against theft or damage.

The other option at 18 (and 16) is to go out and get a job. All jobs are different but there are a few similarities that link them all. The first is tax. We all have to pay tax on our earnings above a certain level – this is currently, for the 1996/97 tax year, £3,765 for a single person (married couples get an extra £1,790). The first £3,900 above this is taxed at 20%, with the remainder to £25,500 taxed at 24%. Above this our income is taxed at 40%. The TAX GUIDE sets out all the main different tax rates.

In addition to tax, National Insurance (NI) is also payable out of our monthly salary. This varies with the amount we earn, but the rule of thumb for basic rate taxpayers is that about a third of your wages is paid in tax and NI each month. National Insurance contributions are paid to entitle us to State benefits such as a pension, invalidity benefit and statutory sick pay. If you have opted out of part of the State pension – the State Earnings Related Pension Scheme (SERPS) – then your NI contributions are reduced. Opting out costs you less and means that the Government will give you a lump sum of money to put into your own pension – see the PERSONAL PENSION GUIDE – but it does mean that you are not entitled to the maximum possible pension from the State on retirement.

Working does have a few perks though. Leaving aside your wages, you are also entitled to join your company's pension scheme and any other schemes such as private health insurance, share options for employees and cheap life insurance. Remember though that any benefits you receive that are given to you by your firm will be taxed as a benefit in kind by the tax office. The different sorts of company pension scheme are explained in the COMPANY PENSION GUIDE.

Companies also offer other different sorts of benefit such as Private Medical Insurance, Permanent Health Insurance (income replacement schemes if you are unable to work for a long time) and Life Insurance. They can do this because most insurance companies will give a discount for bulk buying – as with many other types of retailer – and they can buy it for you cheaper than you could get it on your own.

These perks are either offered to you at the cost of providing them or even cheaper, because the company is paying part of the monthly cost for you. It is worth getting some prices on your own though before signing up for a company scheme, because you may find that you can get the level of cover you need cheaper on your own, rather than paying a standard rate based on the average of all the people you work with. In Section 2 the PRIVATE MEDICAL INSURANCE GUIDE, PERMANENT HEALTH INSURANCE GUIDE and LIFE ASSURANCE GUIDE explain how these insurances work and what you should be looking out for.

Finally, in your teens you are likely to go on holiday without your parents for the first time. Where you go is up to you, but to stop your dream holiday becoming a nightmare it is worth taking out travel insurance. This will cover you if you lose your luggage, passport and travellers' cheques or are injured while abroad. The TRAVEL GUIDE explains how it works and the different types available.

## GUIDES MENTIONED IN CHAPTER ONE

ADVISERS GUIDE
BANK GUIDE
BUILDING SOCIETY GUIDE
CAR GUIDE
COMPANY PENSION GUIDE
HOME INSURANCE GUIDE
LIFE ASSURANCE GUIDE
PERMANENT HEALTH INSURANCE GUIDE
PERSONAL PENSION GUIDE
PRIVATE MEDICAL INSURANCE GUIDE
RENT GUIDE
TAX GUIDE
TRAVEL GUIDE

CHAPTER TWO

# TWENTIES

BY now, you probably have a bank account and will have, or be starting, your first job. If you haven't then it could be worth going back to Chapter One and looking at the guides mentioned there – such as the BANK GUIDE and the PERSONAL PENSION GUIDE.

This age is, hopefully, the fun time. At first, you start to earn enough money to enjoy your new-found freedom, then comes a time to settle down and marry or live with a partner. You might also have children, buy a house and set up some longer term savings. Whatever you do it is likely to cost money.

Since people's needs can differ, this chapter is primarily aimed at single people. Chapter Three deals with the additional areas that come up when you get married or are living with someone.

The biggest purchase you are likely to make is buying your first house. There comes a time for most of us when we are fed up with paying off someone else's mortgage and we want and can afford to buy a place of our own.

If you are perfectly happy renting – or cannot afford to buy a house – then you may want to skip the next few paragraphs until you decide to buy. The RENT GUIDE may be worth a look at though.

Getting the right mortgage is one of the most difficult decision making processes that you go through financially. The wrong decision can cost you a lot of money and, in the case of an endowment policy, be with you for up to 25 years. The MORTGAGE GUIDE sets out the different forms of mortgage – endowment, PEP, pension and repayment. But there are some simple guidelines to follow that will make life a little easier.

Choose what sort of interest you want to pay on your loan – variable, fixed rate or discount. Also, how do you want to repay the loan – via an endowment, pension, PEP or repayment mortgage?

Traditionally, *endowment mortgages* have been the biggest sellers in the mortgage market. This is because until about ten years ago there were only these and repayment mortgages available. Nowadays they are often sold because they are the easiest to explain and give the adviser the biggest amount of money in commission (see the ADVISERS GUIDE for more explanation).

There is nothing wrong with an endowment mortgage whereby you pay off the interest on the loan over the life of the mortgage (normally 25 years) and a monthly amount into the endowment – a savings plan with life cover which pays off the loan at the end of the term. But they are inflexible.

*Personal equity plan* (PEP) mortgages are much more flexible and can be stopped and started at will. But they are riskier than endowments, as your money goes straight into the Stockmarket via unit or investment trusts. (See the UNIT TRUST GUIDE, INVESTMENT TRUST GUIDE and PEP GUIDE for fuller explanations.)

The other interest-only mortgage, as opposed to one that repays interest and capital each month, is a *pension mortgage*. Each month money is paid into your pension and when you retire the lump sum you receive is used to pay off the mortgage.

*Repayment mortgages* are ones where you pay back both the income and capital each month until the loan is paid off. (Also have a look at the HOME INSURANCE GUIDE, which explains about insuring your home and belongings against theft or damage.)

Now is the time that you are likely to start borrowing money to fund other purchases such as a car. There are a variety of different types of loan available from secured or unsecured loans – those that are backed by a car or house, for example – to credit cards or loan sharks.

Both unsecured and secured loans can be arranged through your bank or building society and are explained in the BANK GUIDE and the BUILDING SOCIETY GUIDE. Credit cards and store cards offer another form of loan – the buy now, pay later type. While this can work out cheaper than an overdraft, check how much you actually have to pay each month in interest before you go on a spending spree. The CARD GUIDE sets out how credit cards and store cards work and the things to watch out for.

Buying goods on hire purchase or 'easy terms' is another way to delay paying the full amount at once on expensive items such as cars or washing machines. In a bid to get us to part with our money, shops offer interest-free credit for a fixed period. This is all well and good, but check how much interest you will have to pay after this period is up, and the penalties for repaying early or paying late one month. Sometimes a credit card may work out the cheaper option.

The final form of borrowing, which is included as a warning rather than a recommendation, is that of loan sharks. Rumours of thousands of per cent interest and knee capping if you don't pay up on time are not a million miles from the truth.

If you do need to go to a back-street lender, check that they have an up-to-date Consumer Credit Licence – the Office of Fair Trading in London will do a search for you for a small fee. And get an expert to look over the paperwork for you – if you can't afford to pay or don't know anyone then your local Citizens' Advice Bureau will be able to check it.

Also remember that if you think you are paying too much interest then you can take the lender to court, under the Consumer Credit Act, to have it lowered. Your local Trading Standards Office will be able to help on this one. Remember that the Consumer Credit Act of 1974 only covers loans of up to £15,000.

While you are single with no dependants there is no real need for life insurance – mortgages come with life insurance to pay off the debt should you die before it is paid off. If you do want to take some out then the LIFE ASSURANCE GUIDE explains what is available. But there are other types of cover that you may need such as Permanent Health Insurance (PHI) and Critical Illness Cover (CIC). You may also want to take out Private Medical Insurance, PMI (see the PRIVATE MEDICAL INSURANCE GUIDE), though this is a luxury rather than a necessity.

At any one point in time one million people will have been off work due to sickness for over six months and you are five times more likely to develop a long-term illness than die before the age of 65. Although your company will pay you a certain amount of sick pay it won't last forever, and once the State takes over, many people will see their monthly income fall.

Permanent health insurance replaces your income if you are unable to work for a long period of time. The PERMANENT HEALTH INSURANCE GUIDE explains how it works and the different options available. While the State continues to pay its current levels of income replacement, if you earn less than £15,000, especially if you are married with children, then you probably don't need PHI just yet.

The other type of insurance that pays out if you are ill is critical illness insurance. Unlike PHI it pays out a tax-free lump sum on diagnosis of a range of different conditions such as a heart attack, cancer, multiple sclerosis or permanent disability.

While no one likes to think that it will happen to them, think how many people you know who have suffered a critical illness. The statistics speak for themselves – one in three people in the UK will contract cancer and 90% of these cases will be life threatening. But nearly 50% of women and 33% of men diagnosed as having cancer will still be alive five years later; 150,000 people will have a heart attack this year and 100,000 people a stroke. To top it all, the average age of someone being struck down with a critical illness is just 41, and a quarter of the total are under 35.

How would you cope if you did suffer from one of these illnesses – how would you pay the bills and the mortgage? The CRITICAL ILLNESS INSURANCE GUIDE sets out how this type of insurance works and the types of illness covered. By now the question of a pension will also be getting more urgent. Don't leave it up to chance or the State to provide for you in retirement – neither will do so adequately, if at all. Unless you have a rich aunt or parents who are intending to leave you all their millions, you need a pension.

The first thing to do is to check what your company offers. A personal pension scheme can rarely match the benefits offered by a company or occupational scheme – so if you can join, do so. (The COMPANY PENSION GUIDE explains the different types of scheme on offer.)

If you can't or don't want to join your company scheme, are self-employed or intend to move jobs frequently, then a personal pension will be better for you. This also pays out a lump sum plus an income on retirement but unlike a company scheme moves around jobs with you. Some employers will pay into a personal pension if you choose not to go into a company scheme – or they don't run one – so check all your options before doing anything. The PERSONAL PENSION GUIDE explains how this type of pension works.

If you can afford it, and have enough rainy day money saved, you may also want to start looking at saving money somewhere other than a bank or building society. The Government has created a range of tax-free schemes which are worth looking at to start with.

The oldest of these are National Savings Certificates. These are the

Government's way of borrowing money from you. When you invest in a National Savings Certificate, the Government promises to pay back the money at a date in the future, normally five years. Some of the older certificates – often known as war stock – do not have a repayment date. But because they pay a set level of income they can be bought and sold just like a share.

The interest is set at the beginning and the money can be withdrawn tax free provided you keep it in for the full term. The NATIONAL SAVINGS GUIDE sets out all the different types of National Savings product, from ordinary savings accounts to index-linked bonds and premium bonds.

The first of the more recent Government creations are Personal Equity Plans or PEPs, which were introduced in 1987. These allow you to invest up to £9,000 tax free each year – £6,000 in a qualifying unit or investment trust or share PEP and £3,000 in a single company PEP investing in the shares of just one company. The PEP GUIDE, UNIT TRUST GUIDE, SHARE GUIDE and INVESTMENT TRUST GUIDE explain how these investments work. Once in a PEP, your investment grows tax free, and income and capital gains can be taken from it without paying tax. You can of course invest directly into a unit trust or investment trust – but pay tax – if you prefer.

The other tax-free investment is a TESSA (Tax Exempt Special Saving Account). Over a five-year period you can invest up to £9,000, split £3,000 in year one, £1,800 in years two, three and four and between £600 and £1,800 in year five, depending on how much was invested in year one. The interest rate – or rate of return – varies over the period unless otherwise stated at the outset and the whole lot is tax free if you leave the money untouched for five years. A small amount of income – equivalent to the amount you would have received if the interest had been taxed – can be taken each year without losing the TESSA's tax-free status.

Other types of saving such as investment bonds and SAYE (Save As You Earn) can be found in the BOND GUIDE, BUILDING

SOCIETY GUIDE and FRIENDLY SOCIETY GUIDE. When you are choosing an investment there are two questions to ask yourself before writing any cheques. The first is how much risk am I willing to take – a little or a lot? And also for how long can I afford to tie up my money? Investments such as PEPs and unit trusts are designed for the longer term, at least five years, whereas some bonds can be taken out for just one year.

If you take out a long-term investment but unexpectedly need the money quickly, you may find that you actually lose money because of any penalties, or because the money has not grown as quickly as it would have in a bank account, for example, or an investment that was designed for the short term.

Investments such as shares are risky because the price of the share, such as Marks & Spencer, will go up and down each day. This makes it difficult to get your money back in the short term, as you may have to sell when the price is low regardless of how much you actually paid for it in the first place.

The amount of something you buy will also, to a degree, determine the amount of risk you take. If you put £1,000 into one share it will be riskier than putting that same £1,000 into a unit trust which invests in about 100 different shares. This doesn't make buying individual shares wrong – so long as you know what you are buying.

Finally, if we have missed out any areas that interest you in this chapter then turn to Section 2 – the guides – to find out about them in detail. For example, you may be interested in buying a car and want to know more about car insurance. In this case, the CAR GUIDE should tell you all you need to know. The same goes for holiday insurance – under the TRAVEL GUIDE – and so on.

## GUIDES MENTIONED IN CHAPTER TWO

ADVISERS GUIDE
BANK GUIDE
BOND GUIDE
BUILDING SOCIETY GUIDE
CAR GUIDE
CARD GUIDE
COMPANY PENSION GUIDE
CRITICAL ILLNESS INSURANCE GUIDE
FRIENDLY SOCIETY GUIDE
HOME INSURANCE GUIDE
INVESTMENT TRUST GUIDE
LIFE ASSURANCE GUIDE
MORTGAGE GUIDE
NATIONAL SAVINGS GUIDE
PEP GUIDE
PERMANENT HEALTH INSURANCE GUIDE
PERSONAL PENSION GUIDE
PRIVATE MEDICAL INSURANCE GUIDE
RENT GUIDE
SHARE GUIDE
TRAVEL GUIDE
UNIT TRUST GUIDE

# CHAPTER THREE
# MARRIAGE/LIVING TOGETHER

SO, it's going great. You've met the person of your dreams and you want to move in together, either before or after getting married. There are several ways to do this initially – you move in with them, they move in with you or you buy or rent a totally new place together.

Whatever you do it will involve a change in the money situation. While combining your incomes will give you a lot more disposable income – the bills will also increase. Food bills will almost double and gas and electricity will go up (though probably not by 100%). When you set up home together make sure you set out a few ground rules, as nothing splits up a friendship or a love affair faster than arguments about whose turn it is to pay the telephone bill. Decide who is going to pay what, or if the bills are to be split down the middle, and stick with it.

If you are buying a place together, there are some important questions you should ask before getting a mortgage. Although when you move in you never believe that it is ever going to end, the statistics tell a different story. One in three (and moving rapidly to one in two) marriages end in divorce – ignoring all the people who just live together without ever tying the knot.

While you will probably take out a joint mortgage, it could be worth putting any repayment vehicles – such as an endowment policy – in just one of the names, or make contingency plans for if you split. The MORTGAGE GUIDE sets out the different types of mortgage.

The HOME INSURANCE GUIDE explains the different types of cover you can take out for your possessions. Make sure though that both names are on the deeds or one of you will have no legal right to the property if you split up. If you are not ready to buy your own home yet then it is worth having a look at the RENT GUIDE, which explains the ins and outs of living in rented accommodation.

Many couples find it easier to assign one partner to paying the mortgage and the other all the household bills. Work out what is best for you. Also make sure that you both have enough life cover to pay off the mortgage should one partner die. Endowment policies have built-in life assurance but separate cover has to be taken out with a PEP or pension mortgage. But if, for example, the endowment is in your name, it is worth taking out life cover against your partner's dying, as the last thing you will need if this happens is to worry about paying the mortgage. The LIFE ASSURANCE GUIDE explains the different forms of life cover available.

Lenders will also make you take out mortgage indemnity insurance on loans over 75% of the value of the property – this makes sure that the lender is paid out if you are unable to. But remember this insurance is for the lender, not you, and the insurance company that provided the indemnity insurance can chase you for the money.

To stop yourself falling into arrears through ill health there are several types of insurance that you can take out. The two main ones are Critical Illness Insurance and Permanent Health Insurance. The simplest way to decide whether you need these insurances is to ask yourself two simple questions – how would I cope if my partner or I were unable to work through ill health? And do I have enough capital to pay off the mortgage and provide modifications to the home if they are needed? If the answer to these two questions was no, then you should take out one or other – or both if you can afford it – of these policies.

Critical illness insurance is designed to pay out if you are diagnosed as having one of a range of critical conditions from multiple sclerosis to cancer. The cash lump sum it will give you is tax free and can be used to pay off the mortgage or provide an income – whatever you want. How it works is explained more fully in the CRITICAL ILLNESS INSURANCE GUIDE.

Permanent health insurance is designed to give you an income if you are unable to work. The amount you receive is based on your present income and most will take into account the benefits the State will pay you if you are unable to work, such as a disability allowance and income support. The PERMANENT HEALTH INSURANCE GUIDE explains how this works more fully and sets out the different types of policy available. You can also buy accident, sickness and unemployment cover which normally pays out for a year until State aid kicks in.

While on the theme of medical insurance, if you can afford it Private Medical Insurance, which pays the cost of a private hospital, can also be taken out. The PRIVATE MEDICAL INSURANCE GUIDE sets out this type of cover.

If this is a permanent move leading to marriage or a long-term relationship then there are several other financial steps you may want to take.

Many couples find that setting up a joint bank account is useful for paying the household bills and buying things for both of them. The BANK and BUILDING SOCIETY GUIDES explain about the different types of account available. Before you do this, decide with your partner how much of your wages you will each put in every month – either as a percentage, if you earn vastly different amounts, or as a cash sum.

Do keep your own bank account as well – and make sure that you save some money just for you. The last thing you want to have to do is ask permission to buy something.

Investments tend to be personal things – you can't take out a joint PEP for example. But if you are in a secure relationship then splitting the investments can be tax efficient. If you are married then the Government gives you an extra allowance, above your personal allowance. It is up to you to choose who gets the allowance – based on the most tax saved.

If you are not married (but don't skip this paragraph if you are married, as it is still applicable) there are other ways of reducing your joint tax bill. If only one of you is a higher rate taxpayer then put any investments that provide an income into the other person's name. This is doubly important if one partner does not work, as you could save the full amount in tax. The PEP GUIDE and the NATIONAL SAVINGS GUIDE detail the tax-free options and TESSAs are explained in the BANK and BUILDING SOCIETY GUIDES. It is also worth looking at the UNIT TRUST, INVESTMENT TRUST and SHARE GUIDES for non-tax-free savings.

When you are choosing what to invest in, the three things you must decide are how much you can afford to invest, how long you want to tie your money up for and what level of risk you are comfortable with.

Everything costs money and the art of living well is, to a degree, a matter of knowing your priorities. A little bit of forward planning makes the difference between being able to afford to eat steak if you fancy it, rather than always having to eat chicken.

Forward planning comes into its own when you save for a pension. At 25, 35 or even 45 it is difficult to ever imagine being older and retired – but along with dying it is one of life's certainties. This is why it is so important to have a good pension. A pension should actually be higher on your list of priorities than investments in a PEP or unit trust – though you should make sure you have rainy day money for emergencies, as once invested in a pension the money cannot be touched until you retire.

Before you turn to the nearest insurance salesperson, check out what your work provides. A personal pension will rarely provide such good benefits as those in an occupational or group pension scheme. The COMPANY PENSION GUIDE and the PERSONAL PENSION GUIDE explain how the two different types work. If you are going to take out a personal pension because you intend to move jobs, or your work doesn't provide one, then have a look at the ADVISERS GUIDE before you buy one, as this will explain the different types of advice available.

It is also important to find out about your partner's pension. This will both give you protection if he or she dies, as you will know how much life cover and/or pension you are entitled to, and, if you are married, a guide should it come to divorce and a splitting of assets.

On a nicer note, if you are together in retirement you will have a rough guide to how much income you will have. For unmarried couples, check whether you are entitled to a widow(er)'s pension as a partner not spouse – most companies will allow you to nominate a person to receive the money. If not, make sure you make other arrangements.

On the theme of finding out about your partner, forget whether he or she likes chips or mashed potatoes with sausages – what is his or her financial situation? This may seem a little harsh and calculating, but you would not like to be in the situation of finding that, despite saving your hard-earned cash, you are broke because your partner has spent all the money and run up huge debts.

Also, always take an interest in anything you are asked to sign or put your money into. NEVER sign a document without reading – and more importantly understanding – it first. The horror stories about people who unknowingly signed over their homes as collateral for a business which went bust and were then made homeless are all true.

The final area in this chapter is will writing. Although many people are superstitious and feel that writing a will is tempting fate, it is better to die with your affairs in order than leave a tangled mess for your already distressed friends and family to sort out. See the WILL GUIDE for further guidance.

The laws of the land say that a person's possessions automatically pass to the next of kin – spouse or family – on death, unless otherwise stated. There is no such thing as a common law wife or husband in England and Wales (though there is in Scotland), so if you are in a long-term, unmarried relationship, make sure the will states that you are the beneficiary. The INHERITANCE TAX GUIDE sets out the different ways of reducing an inheritance tax bill on death – but leaving that aside, the last thing you want if you have just lost a loved one is to have to worry about money as well.

Not every area of finance and insurance is covered in each chapter – to do this would make the book about three volumes long. If we have missed out an area in this chapter that you are interested in, such as car insurance or credit cards, then have a look at the guides in Section 2 that relate to those areas. For example, for holiday insurance have a look at the TRAVEL GUIDE and for how store cards work turn to the CARD GUIDE.

## GUIDES MENTIONED IN CHAPTER THREE

ADVISERS GUIDE
BANK GUIDE
BUILDING SOCIETY GUIDE
CARD GUIDE
COMPANY PENSION GUIDE
CRITICAL ILLNESS INSURANCE GUIDE
HOME INSURANCE GUIDE
INHERITANCE TAX GUIDE
INVESTMENT TRUST GUIDE
LIFE ASSURANCE GUIDE
MORTGAGE GUIDE
NATIONAL SAVINGS GUIDE
PEP GUIDE
PERMANENT HEALTH INSURANCE GUIDE
PERSONAL PENSION GUIDE
PRIVATE MEDICAL INSURANCE GUIDE
RENT GUIDE
SHARE GUIDE
TRAVEL GUIDE
UNIT TRUST GUIDE
WILL GUIDE

# CHAPTER FOUR
# CHILDREN

THE gentle sound of pattering feet will be heard by most of us eventually. Some people want children from an early age, others when they have fulfilled certain career objectives, and others not at all. If you fall into the last category then it is probably not worth reading this chapter – unless of course you want to give some helpful hints to a friend who has taken the plunge.

While most of the time they will be worth it, children are expensive. You have to provide for them at least until the age of 16 – legally 18 – and probably for longer than that. The average cost of raising a child to age 16 is over £30,000 – an expensive bundle of joy.

Before you (or your partner) get pregnant – providing it is planned – there is some research you should do. If it is unplanned, still do the research, but the results may be slightly different.

The laws on maternity leave changed on 1 October 1994 – and they have changed in favour of women. A European directive now stops companies from sacking women because they are pregnant – regardless of how long they have worked for the company.

Women should check their rights before they become pregnant. As a rough guide, if they have worked for a company for up to six months, they are allowed 14 weeks' unpaid maternity leave and the company must protect all their benefits such as holidays and any annual bonuses. If they have worked for between six months and two years they are entitled to 14 weeks' maternity leave with up to 18 months' maternity pay. Six weeks of this is at 90% of their current wage, the rest at the State minimum.

If a woman has worked for a firm for more than two years she will be entitled to 40 weeks' maternity leave – 11 before and 29 after the birth – with her benefits protected. Legally, a woman has to be paid for 18 weeks of this by the company, but it will probably pay for longer. If you can delay having a baby until after these various cut-off points then it may be financially worth while. Remember though that there are certain exemptions for smaller companies on maternity leave, so check what applies to your company.

For unmarried parents there are additional benefits you are entitled to. The Inland Revenue produces a useful booklet – 'A Guide for One-Parent Families' (IR92) – which sets out all entitlements and the tax implications.

In this chapter we mostly talk about making joint arrangements with a partner, but single parents need as many of these insurances as those with other halves, so don't skip a paragraph just because it starts with 'you and your partner. . .' The only difference there may be is that a single mother may have less money to spend than if she were part of a couple. As with all the chapters, we have tried to list everything that you could need in an ideal world. But since we don't live in one, the idea is to pick and choose the cover or savings that are right for you and that you can afford on your present salary.

Also if you are interested in a particular topic that we have not covered in this chapter turn to Section 2 and find the relevant guide, such as the RENT GUIDE, FRIENDLY SOCIETY GUIDE or MORTGAGE GUIDE which will cover the subject in detail.

Now is also the time to review your insurance arrangements. Make sure that both you and your spouse or partner, if you have one, have enough life insurance. Add up how much it would cost either of you to live for a few years and/or pay for a nanny/childminder if one of you should die. Or, if you are a single parent, how much your child will need until he or she is able to earn a living. Then add some, as this will not be enough, and make sure you are covered. The LIFE ASSURANCE GUIDE explains how the different forms of cover work.

Also make sure you have an up-to-date will – see the WILL GUIDE for further details and the INHERITANCE TAX GUIDE for ideas on how to reduce the amount of tax payable on your estate when you die. For single parents it is vital that you name a guardian for your child or children in the will, or they could end up being taken into State care as orphans rather than being looked after by the person you wanted.

It is also worth looking at other forms of insurance if you can afford it. The three main medical ones are Critical Illness Cover, Permanent Health (or income replacement) and Private Medical Insurance.

Critical illness cover will pay out a tax-free lump sum on diagnosis of a range of conditions such as cancer or a heart attack and the money can be used to pay off a mortgage, for example. Many lenders offer it as part of a mortgage package but additional cover can be bought separately.

Permanent health insurance, or income replacement, can also be bought in conjunction with a mortgage – or on its own if you don't have one. This pays out a monthly 'wage' if you are unable to work for a long period of time. See the PERMANENT HEALTH INSURANCE GUIDE and CRITICAL ILLNESS INSURANCE GUIDE for more details of this type of cover.

The other type of medical insurance is Private Medical Insurance. This can be taken out to cover just you or your family as well. Most children require at least one spell in hospital during their childhood and this could make the difference between a stressful experience and one of reduced financial worry. See the PRIVATE MEDICAL INSURANCE GUIDE for more details. All three of these medical insurances may be offered through your company, so check this out before signing on the dotted line, as it may be a cheaper option. Also get professional advice before taking anything out. See the ADVISERS GUIDE for details of the type of financial advice available.

Personal accident insurance is also available for both you and your family. This will pay out a lump sum that can be used for hospital bills or put away as an investment if one of you is injured. See the PERSONAL ACCIDENT GUIDE for more details.

All parents want their childen to have a better start in life than they did, and for some this will include a private education. The experts say that the best way to provide for private school fees is to start saving before the child is born. (Some schools are so popular that you have to put your children's names down on the waiting list as soon as they are born, if not before.) If you do want to send your child to a private school then the SCHOOL FEES PLANNING GUIDE lists the various ways of saving. Remember, the longer you leave the planning, the more you will have to pay for yourself – rather than using the interest that has built up. The idea is to make sure that you can still afford to eat while your child is at school – rather than having to scrimp and save every penny.

If you actually have any spare cash that you want to save for your own future, the guides in Section 2 explain the types of saving available. Have a look at the UNIT TRUST GUIDE, INVESTMENT TRUST GUIDE, SHARE GUIDE, BOND GUIDE and PEP GUIDE. But if you want to save for your child's future – or your parents want to put something away for their grandchildren – there are a series of children-only investments.

The first, and most tax efficient, is a National Savings Children's Bonus Bond. This can be bought by anyone over the age of 16 for anyone under the age of 16, and will grow tax free until the child reaches 21 or the bond is cashed in. Alternatively, premium bonds can be bought for a child. While a more haphazard way of saving than the bonus bond, £1 million is available each month and is paid out tax free. See the NATIONAL SAVINGS GUIDE for further details.

There are also a range of children's bank accounts and building society accounts listed in the BANK and BUILDING SOCIETY GUIDES in the next section. These accounts are taken out with you as trustee (in charge of the money) rather than in the child's name.

Investment in a unit or investment trust or directly into shares can also be made for a child, but this again will be in your or your parent's name and liable to tax.

The average person though will not be able to put away money on a regular basis for a child – it will be difficult enough just paying for the household bills. The State does give some help – child benefit is available if the child is under 11, and single mothers will also be given a extra allowance – both of which are tax free.

On a more practical level some lucky women (or men) will have a choice of whether to return to work immediately or take a few years off. But for most, the decision is where to leave the child while you work – with family, a nursery or crèche or a private nanny.

The Government has said that it would like to see a free nursery place for all children – but this dream has not yet become reality and until it does it is up to individuals to make their own provisions. Some people are lucky enough to have a parent or friend who will look after a child during working hours, but the break-up of the family means that the days of a mother or aunt living within easy distance are fast disappearing.

In their place a whole host of alternatives have sprung up. Childminders who will look after a few children normally at their home during the day are available, as are nannies. Nannies differ from childminders, as they will look after the child in your home, and can either be full time and live in, or just come to you during the day.

There are also a limited number of State nursery places, as well as privately run ones for those who can afford it – the cost can be up to £250 a week – and children do have to be over a certain age before they will be accepted. Make sure you check out the childminder, nanny or nursery thoroughly before entrusting them with your baby. They do have to be registered with your local council. Finally, some employers run a crèche for their employees' children.

The final major issue – for women only in this context, as they are the ones who actually have the babies – is the pension. But for both sexes, it is vital to have one and if you haven't, go immediately to the PERSONAL PENSION GUIDE and COMPANY PENSION GUIDE.

Women who have already started funding a pension have two immediate options – either continue to fund it while having children or have a break. Remember, though, that the equivalent male pension for a woman will cost 15% more, as women live longer. While on maternity leave, continuing to fund a pension should not be too much of a problem – by law a company must continue to pay into a scheme (if it did so before pregnancy) even if the mother-to-be can't afford to, or she can take a premium holiday.

But problems can start if a woman decides to take a career break to look after the children while they are small. Since people cannot pay into a pension while they are not working, if they want to have a healthy pension they will have to overfund it when they return to work (and will have already done so if they could afford it and were organised enough before they left full-time employment).

In terms of a State pension, instead of paying National Insurance stamps to fund a State pension on retirement, the Government awards people home responsibility points which reduce the number of years they have to work to get a full State pension by the number of years spent looking after their children.

Things also get more complicated if a person decides to go back to work part-time as the children get older. Fifty per cent of people with a youngest child between the ages of 5 and 9 work part-time, but the rights protecting them are not what they should be.

Check your rights before you start working part-time or job sharing, or you may find that your employer can sack you or make you redundant without having to give you any money or any right to fight back. The European Union has also ruled that part-time workers can join a company pension scheme, so check this out before making your own provisions.

Finally, for both sexes, now you have kids certain other insurances will change. Travel insurance, for example, will have to be extended to cover them – though some policies cover children under a certain age automatically. Also you may be buying a car for the first time. The guides for these two examples are the TRAVEL GUIDE and the CAR GUIDE, but all other aspects of insurance and investments are explained in other guides.

## GUIDES MENTIONED IN CHAPTER FOUR

ADVISERS GUIDE
BANK GUIDE
BOND GUIDE
BUILDING SOCIETY GUIDE
CAR GUIDE
COMPANY PENSION GUIDE
CRITICAL ILLNESS INSURANCE GUIDE
FRIENDLY SOCIETY GUIDE
INHERITANCE TAX GUIDE
INVESTMENT TRUST GUIDE
LIFE ASSURANCE GUIDE
MORTGAGE GUIDE
NATIONAL SAVINGS GUIDE
PEP GUIDE
PERMANENT HEALTH INSURANCE GUIDE
PERSONAL ACCIDENT GUIDE
PERSONAL PENSION GUIDE
PRIVATE MEDICAL INSURANCE GUIDE
RENT GUIDE
SCHOOL FEES PLANNING GUIDE
SHARE GUIDE
TRAVEL GUIDE
UNIT TRUST GUIDE
WILL GUIDE

## CHAPTER FIVE
# DIVORCE

SADLY, one in three marriages ends in divorce, and for those who live together but do not marry the figures are even worse. This chapter deals with divorce only, as sadly people who live together do not have the same automatic rights as married people when they split.

That said, if you do decide to live together and not marry then it is worth getting a document drawn up and witnessed, stating what each person brings to the partnership and – if you can – how you would like things to be divided if you split. If children are involved then your partner will have an enforceable legal obligation to pay maintenance towards the child's upkeep, but not to yours.

The first thing to do in a divorce is to get yourself a solicitor. Your best bet is to find one who specialises in family law.

The next thing is to inform your bank or building society and ask them only to accept instructions with both your names on it, freeze the account, or check with you before allowing large sums of money to be withdrawn. This also applies to any joint credit cards which could be worth freezing or you can ask for a separate one to be issued in your name only. The last thing you need is your spouse moving all your joint money into a secret account or running up huge debts for which you are jointly liable. Remember that while you are not liable for your spouse's debts, you are liable for any joint debts or borrowings such as the mortgage.

If you don't have a bank or building society account – as your spouse has traditionally arranged the family finances and given you an allowance – then set one up. The BANK and BUILDING SOCIETY GUIDES list what is available and the different sorts of account.

While you are in informing mode, it is also worth telling your mortgage lender if you think that you will have problems meeting the monthly payments. If you let your lender know before you fall into arrears then the more chance there is that you can reschedule payments or come to some sort of agreement which lets you off the hook until you have sorted out your finances. You may also be able to suspend any regular payments to a pension or savings scheme until you are sorted out. But don't stop paying into life assurance policies – especially those on your spouse's life. This also applies to any home contents, car or building contents insurance. The last thing you need is to have an accident in your car and/or have a fire or be burgled at home if you are not covered.

The next thing to do is to take a deep breath and sit down and work out what you will need in the way of income and capital to live on – before you start negotiating any divorce settlement. Find out what you are entitled to from the State; your local DSS office will give you an idea as to which sorts of benefits you can get -- such as an extra allowance for being a single parent if you have children. If you can, put off making any long-term financial decisions until you are calm and able to think clearly.

The same thing applies to the person who will be supporting his or her ex-spouse. Work out what you think he or she needs to live on, and what you think you will need to live on once you are divorced.

There is no point in agreeing to large maintenance payments if you know that there is no way you can afford them. The more proof you have about both your costs of living, the stronger your case will be to get a manageable settlement.

The best way to work out what you will need is to write down all your income and outgoings each month. If you don't know, have a month with a notebook jotting down everything you spend as you spend it. Section 3 contains a wealth check which lists all the sorts of income and outgoings you may have and lets you fill in your own individual amounts.

Also list all your and your spouse's assets. Don't forget things like pension schemes and any savings you think he or she may have. Remember that once you divorce you have no entitlement to either your ex-spouse's personal or company pension scheme. While the law in this country does not yet give you any legal entitlement to any part of your soon-to-be ex-spouse's pension on retirement, it can be taken into account when awarding the settlement.

With the State pension, you are allowed to use your ex-spouse's employment record to provide you with a pension if you do not have enough National Insurance stamps in your own right – or he or she just has more. This option stops, though, if you remarry – then you must use the employment record of your new spouse. If, however, you are already drawing a State pension based on your ex-spouse's employment record when you remarry, then you keep your ex-spouse's one.

While you are working out how much money you will need, don't forget that inflation will erode the value of any payments over the longer term. Also, since your spouse may not be able to afford the amount you ideally need, work out the minimum amount you could exist on if you cut out all the extras such as charity donations and exotic foreign holidays.

If you have children then the chances are your ex-spouse will be ordered by the courts to pay maintenance each month towards their upkeep. If they are at private schools, don't forget to include the fees – if they are paid by your spouse – in any settlement.

If your spouse dies while still paying maintenance then the payments will stop at the time of death. Make sure that he or she has adequate life cover with you as the named beneficiary to cover the payments – which will normally last until the children finish school or full-time education. The LIFE ASSURANCE GUIDE explains how life cover works and the different types.

Maintenance payments are tax free – though you have to include them on your income tax return – and any payment made specifically to your children must be invested on their behalf.

Also remember that any maintenance payments to you – rather than the children – will probably stop if you get remarried (depending on your divorce settlement). And if you receive the family home as part of the settlement, make sure that your spouse's name is taken off the deeds, with yours remaining as the sole owner.

As a final note, the Child Support Act 1991, which came into force in April 1993, allows you to apply to the Child Support Agency if you are not receiving the maintenance granted to you, or it is not enough and you need the amount increased. If you are claiming or about to claim money from the State (eg. income support, family credit, disability working allowance) then the DSS will automatically refer you to the Child Support Agency.

Once the details of the divorce settlement are finalised and you have celebrated (or commiserated) with champagne and caviare that you are now free and single again, it is time to start thinking about the longer term.

Put any money you received in the settlement into a high-interest bank or building society account until you have decided what to do. Getting good financial advice at this point is a must. The ADVISERS GUIDE in the next section sets out the different types of advice available to you.

If you received cash as part of the settlement then this will need to be invested for both income now and capital growth in the future. An adviser will be able to tell you what is the best combination for your particular circumstances but the UNIT TRUST, INVESTMENT TRUST, SHARE, PEP and NATIONAL SAVINGS GUIDES will give you a rough idea. Also read the BOND GUIDE and FRIENDLY SOCIETY GUIDE as well as the BANK and BUILDING SOCIETY GUIDES for shorter term savings, low-risk and rainy day money.

It could be worth paying off the mortgage on your home or reducing the loan down to £30,000 with the money and getting the maximum tax relief. Again an adviser will be able to tell you the best course of action for your circumstances.

As mentioned above, once divorced you lose all entitlement to your spouse's pension and any other employee perks such as Private Medical Insurance that he or she receives. The most important one of these to replace is the pension. If you are working then find out about any pension scheme your company runs – remember part-time workers are eligible – or seek advice on a good personal pension. The PERSONAL PENSION and COMPANY PENSION GUIDES explain how a pension works. It is also worth finding out what State pension you have from your local benefits office. If you are not working, there are other tax-efficient savings you can make to act as a quasi-pension on retirement – ask your adviser and see the savings guides mentioned above. If you do work, but do not earn enough to pay tax, the personal pension route is still open to you.

If you can afford it then there are other forms of insurance that are worth looking at. These are medical insurances such as private health insurance, critical illness insurance, permanent health (income replacement) insurance and personal accident cover for both you and your children, if you have any. PMI – explained in the PRIVATE MEDICAL INSURANCE GUIDE – is probably the least urgent of the other insurances, but it does entitle you to instant private health care should you need it. See the CRITICAL ILLNESS INSURANCE and PERMANENT HEALTH INSURANCE GUIDES for further details.

The other insurance worth taking out is personal accident insurance – for both you and any children. As with all of the insurances mentioned in this book, whether you take them out is dependent on the amount of cover you can afford and, in some cases, actually need. The full range of insurances are dealt with within this book, as some will suit you and not another person, and vice versa. In an ideal world we would all be able to afford to cover ourselves fully against every eventuality – but we don't live in an ideal world.

Back to personal accident insurance. Like critical illness it will pay out a lump sum, but this time if you have an accident. While insuring any children against accidents may seem an odd concept, one in five children are involved in accidents that require hospital treatment each year and 120,000 are hospitalised.

If they are badly injured then you may have to take time off work to nurse them or adapt the home to allow for any permanent disability. Now you are the only breadwinner it is important to protect yourself against these unexpected costs. The PERSONAL ACCIDENT GUIDE explains what is available.

If you find that you need to, there are a variety of ways of borrowing money. The easiest is through your bank or building society – explained in the relevant guides in the next section. Remember that an authorised overdraft is much cheaper than an unauthorised one and it pays to keep your bank manager informed if you do need to borrow. You can also borrow on a credit card or store card (explained in the CARD GUIDE) or through hire purchase or 'easy terms' – whereby you pay a little each month. This can work out more expensive though, so check the terms and conditions before you sign on the dotted line.

Also look at the interest-free credit terms given by many retailers on larger purchases. They can be a good idea, but read the small print and find out about the hidden charges levied on late payments or early repayment, for example.

The most drastic way of borrowing money is to go to a loan shark. This is not advisable – please exhaust every other avenue, including local credit unions and your local council, before doing this. But if you cannot get money through any other means, have the paperwork read by someone qualified before you do anything. Your local Citizens' Advice Bureau will be able to help if you do not know anyone else.

Also remember that if you are, or think you are, paying too much interest you can apply to the courts, under the Consumer Credit Act, to have it lowered. Your local Trading Standards Office will be able to help on this one. The Consumer Credit Act is only applicable for loans under £15,000 though.

Now you are on your own you may also have to deal with other financial products that were previously dealt with by your ex-spouse. If this is the case then it is worth reading the CAR GUIDE, TRAVEL GUIDE and HOME INSURANCE GUIDE in the next section of the book. If you are forced to move home then the MORTGAGE GUIDE and/or the RENT GUIDE may make useful reading.

The final step is to make sure that you have an up-to-date will. If you don't you could die intestate and either end up leaving everything to the State or make it difficult for your friends and relatives to unlock the money. If your ex-spouse has ongoing commitments to you, make sure these are provided for in his or her will, as well as any life insurance with you as beneficiary – written in trust. The WILL GUIDE and TRUST GUIDE explain how these are done.

If you are in receipt of a lot of money from the divorce, it is also worth ensuring that you make some sort of arrangements to reduce the amount of inheritance tax that will be payable on your money and property should you die. The various ways of doing this are given in the INHERITANCE TAX GUIDE.

## GUIDES MENTIONED IN CHAPTER FIVE
ADVISERS GUIDE
BANK GUIDE
BOND GUIDE
BUILDING SOCIETY GUIDE
CAR GUIDE
CARD GUIDE
COMPANY PENSION GUIDE
CRITICAL ILLNESS INSURANCE GUIDE
FRIENDLY SOCIETY GUIDE
HOME INSURANCE GUIDE
INHERITANCE TAX GUIDE
INVESTMENT TRUST GUIDE
LIFE ASSURANCE GUIDE
MORTGAGE GUIDE
NATIONAL SAVINGS GUIDE
PEP GUIDE
PERMANENT HEALTH INSURANCE GUIDE
PERSONAL ACCIDENT GUIDE
PERSONAL PENSION GUIDE
PRIVATE MEDICAL INSURANCE GUIDE
RENT GUIDE
SHARE GUIDE
TRAVEL GUIDE
TRUST GUIDE
UNIT TRUST GUIDE
WILL GUIDE

CHAPTER SIX

# MIDDLE AGE

RUMOUR has it that middle age is the best time of your life – all those birthday cards telling you that life begins at 40 must be true! Joking aside though, there is no reason why these should not be the best years of your life. The kids have moved out (if you had any) and it is now time for you (and your spouse or partner if you have one) to start enjoying life again – a bit like being 20 but hopefully with more money to spend.

This chapter deals with what the financial services industry terms 'empty nesters' – people in their forties or fifties who have grown-up children – who have now moved away – and who have a higher percentage of disposable income than at any other point in the life cycle. If your children haven't yet moved out, have a read anyway, as there are some things that apply to the age group as well as the lifestyle.

So the kids have finally left – no more school fees to pay, sandwiches to make and new computers, clothes and extra food to buy. Suddenly the pay packet stretches further – even after the exotic food and drink you can now afford to buy – and you may actually have money left at the end of the month. Deciding what to do with it has got to be one of life's tougher decisions!

In terms of financial products, now is the time to think longer term about health policies and making sure you have enough money in a pension or savings to provide for a comfortable retirement. As with the other chapters we are going to go through the whole spectrum of financial services you could possibly need – pick and choose what suits both your lifestyle and pocket. That said, if there is an area you are interested in that we have not touched on in this chapter, such as credit cards, turn to the next section and find the guide that relates to the topic. In the example above the CARD GUIDE tells you all you need to know about both credit cards and store cards.

The urgency of making sure you have an adequately funded pension really comes to the fore at this time. We cannot stress how important having a decent pension is. Having worked all your life and worried about money for 60-odd years, the last thing you want is to have to worry until your dying day about whether you can afford to turn the heating on when it is snowing outside.

Making your own pension provisions puts you in the driving seat and able to decide when you retire, rather than being forced to work until you are too old to enjoy not having to get up for work, because of money worries.

The first thing to do is to check how much pension you actually have. Your local Social Security office will have the booklet NP38 'Your Future Pension' which has an application form to get the information about your State pension. If you have paid into a company or personal pension scheme, find out how much you have in it and what your pension is estimated to be on retirement. The PERSONAL PENSION and COMPANY PENSION GUIDES in the next section explain what these are and how they work.

If you have lots of small amounts of money in different company pension schemes – run by the different companies you have worked for – it may be worth transferring them into your current scheme. Before you do this, check with a financial adviser as to the penalties of moving the money. Some schemes have such high transfer costs, or the benefits are so much better in them than your current scheme, that you may lose out financially. The ADVISERS GUIDE lists the different types of advice available.

If there is not enough money in your pension(s) then you should start paying in more. The simplest question to ask yourself, if you are unsure about funding levels, is how much income will I realistically need to survive on comfortably in retirement? It will probably be less than while you are working, as costs such as commuting to and from work and a separate wardrobe of working clothes will no longer be needed.

At this relatively late stage a pension will cost a lot. If you have a cash lump sum, putting it in a pension is one of the most tax-efficient ways of saving – as the Government gives tax relief on contributions. This means that as a standard rate taxpayer, for every £76 you put in the Government will put in £24.

Alternatively, you could invest your money in a Personal Equity Plan (PEP). While there is no tax relief on contributions into a PEP, the money grows tax free and can be taken tax free as an income or lump sum whenever you want. A pension can only be taken when you retire, or are over a certain age – most pension schemes set this at between age 50 and 75. The PEP GUIDE explains about this form of saving and it may be a cheaper alternative for people who have not yet made pension provisions.

If you do want to continue down the pensions route there are several options. The first is to increase the amount you pay in each month. The second for company scheme members is to pay into a policy called an additional voluntary contribution scheme (AVC). There are two types of these – an AVC run alongside your company pension scheme with the insurance company chosen by your employer, or a free-standing AVC (FSAVC) – one that is not directly linked to your company scheme. These are run by most insurance companies and you should get advice as to which is the best for you. How they both work is explained in the AVC AND FSAVC GUIDE in the next section.

The other thing to check is that you have enough health care insurance and life assurance on your partner's life, and he or she on yours, in the event of an untimely death. The LIFE ASSURANCE GUIDE explains how life cover works and the different policies available.

Unfortunately, the older you get, the more likely you are to become ill – and because of this the cost of health care insurance increases. The two main types are critical illness insurance and private medical insurance. The Private Medical Insurance – explained in the PRIVATE MEDICAL INSURANCE GUIDE in the next section – will pay for private health care if you get ill. It will also give cash payments if you go into an NHS hospital.

Critical illness insurance, on the other hand, will pay out a cash lump sum if you are diagnosed as having a range of critical conditions, from a heart attack or stroke to loss of sight. This insurance is explained further in the CRITICAL ILLNESS INSURANCE GUIDE.

You may also want to protect yourself in the last years of your working life with an income replacement policy which will pay out a wage each month if you are unable to work due to sickness or disability. This is explained in the PERMANENT HEALTH INSURANCE GUIDE in the next section.

There is another health-type insurance you should be thinking about in your middle years and this is long-term care insurance. Most people will have had some experience of the problems old age brings by now, through their parents or relatives.

If you haven't, here are the statistics. We, in Britain, are an ageing population – by 2040 only a quarter of the population will be working to support the other three-quarters. By the year 2001 there will be 12 million people in Britain over the age of 60 – and by 2041 over 50% of the elderly population will be over 75 as compared with 44% in 1991.

The net effect will be that: a) there will not be enough people funding the social security system to afford to pay out all the State pensions required – hence the need to make private provisions; and b) there will not be enough carers – children or other relatives – able and willing to look after an elderly parent or relative.

The problem is compounded by the cost to the State of looking after an elderly person. For every £1 the NHS spends on someone under 65, £4 is spent on someone over this age. The Government also spent £1,872m in 1991 on income support costs for people in nursing or residential homes alone, and the cost is rising rapidly each year. Compare this with a background of reducing services and funding for the NHS and the problem looks even more serious.

But there is a way of avoiding this dilemma. This is by taking out long-term care insurance – a way of funding the cost of a stay in a long-term nursing or residential home, or home nursing. But it is expensive unless you start thinking about it in your 40s or 50s. The different ways of funding are explained in the LONG-TERM CARE GUIDE in the next section and it is important to make your own provisions.

On a nicer note you may want to use the extra cash you have in these years to buy a second holiday home somewhere in the sun. You cannot get tax relief on a mortgage – known as MIRAS – on two houses (except if you are actively trying to sell one, in which case double MIRAS relief is available for up to a year). But you do have the choice of which home you tell the Inland Revenue is your main property, so you can switch the relief if there is a greater saving to you, or get tax relief if you have already paid off the mortgage on your existing house.

As an aside, you may want to increase the payments on your existing mortgage, or pay it off completely if you have a cash lump sum. But if you have an endowment attached, think very carefully about surrendering it, as you may lose an awful lot of money encashing it with only a few years to go. If you do want to get rid of it, contact the Association of Policy Market Makers whose members will buy it off you at, on average, about 30% more than the value the insurance company will give if you surrender it. Remember, though, you can pay off the mortgage loan and still continue paying into the endowment.

If you are thinking about buying a second home, moving house or making home improvements, the MORTGAGE GUIDE in the next section explains the different types and the BANK and BUILDING SOCIETY GUIDES detail the different types of loan available if you do not want to increase your mortgage for home improvement. Also read the HOME INSURANCE GUIDE, which details the different types of home contents and buildings insurance you need.

Alternatively, you may just want to save any extra cash you have. The UNIT TRUST, INVESTMENT TRUST and SHARE GUIDES explain ways of investing in the Stockmarket with varying degrees of risk while the BOND GUIDE, NATIONAL SAVINGS GUIDE and FRIENDLY SOCIETY GUIDE explain safer investment alternatives.

Reaching 50 has a variety of perks ranging from cheaper car insurance to being able to retire. Car insurance is cheaper because people over 50 are deemed to be better and safer drivers. The CAR GUIDE sets out how this insurance works.

People over 50 also get their own type of travel insurance – see the TRAVEL GUIDE – which, while it can be more expensive, places more emphasis on health cover than loss of luggage, for example.

The final issues to address are making a will and inheritance tax planning. You must have an up-to-date will or it is highly likely that you will end up leaving your hard-earned possessions to the State, not your loved ones – especially if you are not married. See the WILL GUIDE for more details.

The other thing for both yourself and your parents, if they are still alive, to think about is inheritance tax (IHT) planning. If you have lost a parent you may know a little about it, but the INHERITANCE TAX

GUIDE sets out all the different rules and ways round paying it. It is known as the voluntary tax, as most people will not have enough to leave to meet the current £200,000 threshold or plan their affairs so as to avoid paying it.

While working out how to reduce your potential inheritance tax liability, you may need to set up a life policy written in trust. The TRUST GUIDE sets out the different sorts of trust available and how they can be used to benefit you and your family.

## GUIDES MENTIONED IN CHAPTER SIX

ADVISERS GUIDE

AVC AND FSAVC GUIDE

BANK GUIDE

BOND GUIDE

BUILDING SOCIETY GUIDE

CAR GUIDE

CARD GUIDE

COMPANY PENSION GUIDE

CRITICAL ILLNESS INSURANCE GUIDE

FRIENDLY SOCIETY GUIDE

HOME INSURANCE GUIDE

INHERITANCE TAX GUIDE

INVESTMENT TRUST GUIDE

LIFE ASSURANCE GUIDE

LONG-TERM CARE GUIDE

MORTGAGE GUIDE

NATIONAL SAVINGS GUIDE

PEP GUIDE

PERMANENT HEALTH INSURANCE GUIDE

PERSONAL PENSION GUIDE

PRIVATE MEDICAL INSURANCE GUIDE

SHARE GUIDE

TRAVEL GUIDE

TRUST GUIDE

UNIT TRUST GUIDE

WILL GUIDE

# CHAPTER SEVEN
# RETIREMENT

WELL, you've made it. No more getting up for work every morning, standing in packed commuter trains, traffic jams, taking the children to school – or doing pretty much anything you don't want to. Now should be your time to eat smoked salmon and caviare for every meal, if you want to. If you haven't made any provisions for your retirement, don't despair – there are still some things you can do to increase your income.

The first thing to do is to activate your pension – turn it into an income for you to live on. If you have a company scheme, explained in the COMPANY PENSION GUIDE, then they will already have told you how much money you have. The same applies to a personal pension, explained in the PERSONAL PENSION GUIDE. If you haven't been told yet then find out, and make sure that you get details of all the different pension schemes you have ever paid into, however long ago, as the money is still yours. Contact the Pensions Schemes Registry to track down any lost plans. This includes any money you may have paid into an additional voluntary contributions scheme (AVC) or free-standing AVC (known as an FSAVC) to boost your retirement income. These schemes, explained in detail in the AVC AND FSAVC GUIDE, basically run alongside your main pension and allow you to top up the amount you put in each year, thus increasing your final pension.

Both types of pension will allow you to take part as a tax-free lump sum – a personal pension limits this to 25% of the total fund – with the remainder used to buy an annuity to fund regular income payments, based on the current interest rates. Alternatively, you can use the full amount to buy an annuity and have a bigger monthly income.

An annuity is a policy which guarantees to pay you a fixed amount each month until you die – though annuities that increase in line with inflation, or by a fixed percentage, are available. It stops on your death, so if you live longer than the insurance company estimates then it is out of pocket, and if you die before then you have lost out. An annuity forms no part of your estate on death, unlike the tax-free lump sum. The ANNUITY GUIDE explains how these policies work and the different types available.

You can use the cash lump sum for whatever you like. If you do use it to pay off your mortgage, think very carefully before you surrender any endowment policies that are attached. You may find that the amount you get by surrendering a few years early is vastly smaller than the amount you would get on maturity. Pay off the loan but keep the endowment going if you can afford to. If you can't, think about selling it on as an alternative. The Association of Policy Market Makers can give you more details about this.

On the subject of homes, if you do decide to move to a smaller home or a different area or buy a second holiday home, the MORTGAGE GUIDE in the next section explains the different types of mortgage available, while the BANK and BUILDING SOCIETY GUIDES detail other forms of loan you may need for home improvements, for example.

If you don't own your own home or wish to sell it and move into rented accommodation, then have a look at the RENT GUIDE in the next section.

To advise you on the pension decisions you will have to make – and other financial decisions – it is worth seeking the help of a financial adviser. The ADVISERS GUIDE in the next section explains the types of advice available and what to expect.

You will also become eligible for the State pension, made up of two parts: the basic State pension and the earnings related top-up, known as SERPS. Unfortunately though for women, if they paid the reduced cost Married Women's National Insurance stamps, or have not paid enough National Insurance stamps, then they have no pension entitlement until their husband retires.

If you are divorced and have not remarried then you are entitled to use your ex-spouse's contributions record in place of your own incomplete one to get a better State pension.

As stated above, the second part of the State pension is made up of the State Earnings Related Pension Scheme (SERPS), which is linked to the amount of years you have worked and National Insurance you have paid. It is this part of the State pension that the Government has been encouraging younger people to opt out of for the past few years. Your company may have opted out of SERPS on your behalf, so it is worth checking before you start correspondence with the DSS.

In addition to your pension, the Government also gives you an age allowance, which is a higher starting point for paying income tax when you reach 65, and a further increase at 75. Remember that you will have to pay tax on your pension and any other income you receive from savings. The only tax-free savings are PEPs, TESSAs and some National Savings – which are explained in the PEP GUIDE, BANK and BUILDING SOCIETY GUIDES and the NATIONAL SAVINGS GUIDE.

Once the pension side of things is sorted out and you know exactly how much income you have coming in each month, then you can start to look at some of the other types of saving and insurance.

To work out exactly how much spare cash, if any, you have, it is worth completing the wealth check in the third section of the book. This lists all your possible income and outgoings and allows you to fill in the bits that apply to you. By adding all your income and subtracting the outgoings you can see what is left. If there isn't any, it may highlight any areas of unnecessary spending or overspending which can be cut down or cut out totally.

If you need the capital you have to live on then the last thing you want to do is to put it all in a high-risk investment. The aim is to spread the risk and look for low-risk products. One of the best around is an investment bond. Many companies offer ones that guarantee a fixed level of income or growth over a one- to five-year period (or longer) and guarantee that you will get your money back – if not more – at the end. These, and other types of bond, are explained in the BOND GUIDE in the next section. The Government also offers its own version of this, so have a look at the NATIONAL SAVINGS GUIDE as well.

If you are willing and financially able to take some risk then you may want to invest your money on the Stock Exchange via some form of collective investment, or direct into shares if you have the time and inclination. The UNIT TRUST, INVESTMENT TRUST and SHARE GUIDES explain how to invest in the Stockmarket and the PEP GUIDE shows a tax-free way of doing so.

Holding money in cash is both the safest and the riskiest form of investment. This is because while you are not, potentially, going to see the value plummet overnight – as with shares – its value is slowly eroded by inflation over the years. Plus you are missing out on the higher returns available elsewhere.

That said, it is important to have some money held on deposit or in a high-interest account for emergencies or buying a new car or holiday. The BANK, FRIENDLY SOCIETY and BUILDING SOCIETY GUIDES explain the different types of account available. Cover for your car and any holidays you may go on are explained in the CAR GUIDE and TRAVEL GUIDE in the next section of the book.

As you grow older the different types of insurance you need also change. There is no need for redundancy insurance or one that replaces income if you are unable to work, but you may need one that pays for the cost of long-term care or a stay in hospital.

Unfortunately, the insurances you need also become more expensive as you get older – as you are more likely to claim on them. But they are still worth taking out, as the cost of not being covered will probably be far greater than the extra cost of premiums. The first thing to do is to check that you have enough life cover – both for yourself and as the beneficiary on your spouse or partner's life and vice versa. The LIFE ASSURANCE GUIDE explains how the cover works.

Critical illness insurance is still a good idea though many companies stop the policy at age 65. Your financial adviser will be able to tell you what is still available and the CRITICAL ILLNESS INSURANCE GUIDE in the next section explains how it works.

It is also worth finding out about the cost of private medical insurance, which pays for private treatment and hospitalisation if it is needed. Things like hip replacement and eye surgery can be had much more quickly via this route and it is explained more fully in the PRIVATE MEDICAL INSURANCE GUIDE in the next section.

Probably the most important insurance now is long-term care insurance. This will fund the cost of nursing or residential home fees if you become unable to look after yourself. If you want, it will also pay for a nurse to come to your home. The LONG-TERM CARE GUIDE explains the different types of scheme. While you may not want to think about ever becoming old and infirm, unfortunately it will happen and it is better to be prepared than to become a burden to your family and friends.

On a nicer note, you (and your partner or spouse) may have grandchildren by now and are reliving the joys of having small children around – though you can give them back this time if you want to!

To help them and your son or daughter, you may want to give each child some money. The Government gives all sorts of tax breaks to grandparents doing this. You can help with school fees payments or just set aside money – preferably in trust – for them when they are older. If you give the money directly to the child, rather than via the parents, then you can take advantage of his or her personal tax allowance. If you give it to the parents, who then spend it on behalf of the children, it is treated as their income and is taxed.

You may also be looking at giving money to people as gifts to reduce your inheritance tax liabilities. While this is explained in full in the INHERITANCE TAX GUIDE, you can currently give one person up to £3,000 a year tax free and other people individual gifts of £250 a year. You can also put money aside for someone via a trust, for example, or as a gift, and if you live for seven years thereafter it is free of inheritance tax. See the TRUST GUIDE for ways of writing policies in trust – which have the effect of putting the money or property outside your estate when you die.

While on the unpleasant subject of death, make sure that you have an up-to-date will. Don't die intestate and leave your family and friends the added problem of sorting out your finances when they have enough other problems to cope with. The WILL GUIDE in the next section should help in writing one.

So far this chapter has dealt only with those people fortunate enough to have an adequate pension and savings – but there are a frightening proportion of people who are forced to rely on the State for their income.

If you are in this situation, through a lack of pension planning or because you divorced late in life without having anything set aside or left after the settlement, there are several things you can do to boost the amount of money you receive each month.

If you own a house then it could be time to unlock the cash tied up in the bricks and mortar without having to move out. This is done through a policy called a home income plan. While there has been a lot of bad publicity about these types of scheme in recent years, there are some good ones around that will not leave you vulnerable to eviction.

Home income plans, explained in detail in the HOME INCOME PLAN GUIDE, basically allow you to take out a loan against your house (like a mortgage) while still letting you live in the house until you die. The money raised against the house is invested to provide you with an income during your lifetime and it is only when you die that the house becomes the property of the company that lent you the money.

You have the choice of taking a loan against the full value of your house or only part of it – whichever you do, make sure you tell your family that you are doing it or they may get a nasty shock when your will is read and they realise the house is not included.

Things are more difficult if you do not own your house. The bank or building society will probably be reluctant to give you a loan – though it is worth a try. Or try asking relatives or friends if they will stand as guarantor for the loan – to be paid back after you die with any money that can be raised from selling your possessions. The only catch of course is that the value of your possessions may not be as much as the value of the loan, which means the person acting as guarantor will have to pay the difference – so be realistic when estimating what your possessions are worth.

As an alternative, see if a friend or relative will lend you money to be paid back – in full or as near as possible if they don't mind – on your death. The final option, once you become unable to look after yourself, is to get yourself placed in a residential or nursing home. Your local authority is in charge of allocating places, so speak to the local council, social security office or your doctor to find out whether you are eligible and for help in arranging this.

If you need to borrow money for urgent purchases, for example if your fridge has broken and is beyond repair, it is worth talking to your local council before turning to the nearest loan shark. If this is not an option and you have no other way of borrowing money, then there is the back-street option.

If you have to see a loan shark then make sure you get someone qualified to read over the terms of the contract before you sign anything. If you don't know anyone or cannot afford to pay then your local Citizens' Advice Bureau will be able to help. They are also good places to visit before you go to the loan shark, as they may be able to suggest other alternatives.

Also check that they have an up-to-date Consumer Credit Licence – the Office of Fair Trading in London will do a search for you for a small fee. If you think you are being charged too much interest then you can take your lender to court, under the Consumer Credit Act, to have it lowered. Your local Trading Standards Office will be able to help with this one. Remember that the Consumer Credit Act only covers loans up to £15,000.

# GUIDES MENTIONED IN CHAPTER SEVEN

ADVISERS GUIDE
ANNUITY GUIDE
AVC AND FSAVC GUIDE
BANK GUIDE
BOND GUIDE
BUILDING SOCIETY GUIDE
CAR GUIDE
COMPANY PENSION GUIDE
CRITICAL ILLNESS INSURANCE GUIDE
FRIENDLY SOCIETY GUIDE
HOME INCOME PLAN GUIDE
INHERITANCE TAX GUIDE
INVESTMENT TRUST GUIDE
LIFE ASSURANCE GUIDE
LONG-TERM CARE GUIDE
MORTGAGE GUIDE
NATIONAL SAVINGS GUIDE
PEP GUIDE
PERSONAL PENSION GUIDE
PRIVATE MEDICAL INSURANCE GUIDE
RENT GUIDE
SHARE GUIDE
TRAVEL GUIDE
TRUST GUIDE
UNIT TRUST GUIDE
WILL GUIDE

## CHAPTER EIGHT
# BEREAVEMENT

COPING with the death of a loved one is difficult whatever the age of the person. So it makes sense to make sure that there is the minimum amount of financial worry for the survivors, leaving them to mourn in peace without additional problems.

This chapter deals with the financial aspects of death and lists the things that you can do to make sorting out your estate easier for the people you leave behind.

When people die two things can happen to their estate (their property) – either a will has been written and the estate minus any inheritance tax is paid out, or they die intestate, which technically means everything belongs to the State.

If a person has a will this has to be granted probate, via the Probate Registry, before it can be paid out. If there is no will then you will have to apply for Letters of Administration – like probate – before you can sort out the estate. Remember that any bank accounts the person may have had in his or her own name will be frozen until probate is granted, so make sure, if it is your partner or spouse who has died, that you have access to cash.

The first thing you will have to do is pay inheritance tax of 40% on the estate if the value is more than £200,000 (1996/97 tax year) – though transfers between spouses are inheritance tax free. Although the bulk will have to be paid immediately, tax on certain possessions such as property and land can be deferred for six months after the death and then paid in instalments over ten years or until they are paid.

Gifts given over seven years before death are also inheritance tax free and a sliding scale of tax for gifts given between three and seven years before is applied by the Inland Revenue. The INHERITANCE TAX GUIDE in the next section details both ways to avoid paying inheritance tax and the different possessions it is payable on.

Once the will is sorted out, any life assurance polices such as the life cover included in your mortgage endowment policy will pay up. This should allow the mortgage and hopefully any other debts to be paid off.

If it is your spouse or partner who has just died, things are not as straightforward for you after this. While the loss of an elderly parent or friend is upsetting, it should not affect you financially in the way the death of your spouse or partner will.

Sadly, people who have not married, though lived with their partners as if married, are not automatically entitled to their partner's estate on death unless it says so in the will. This is why a will is so important, and if you don't have one read the WILL GUIDE and make one as soon as possible.

If your spouse, and in some cases partner, has a pension – either company or personal – then you should also be entitled to some money on his or her death. Check with the trustees of the pension scheme to see what you are entitled to. If your partner or spouse was already drawing a pension you may also be entitled to a reduced amount each month. Each scheme is different, so check with the individual employer or provider. The COMPANY PENSION and PERSONAL PENSION GUIDES explain in detail how these sorts of scheme work if you want some background knowledge – or want to set up your own to provide for your retirement.

If you or your children have been left money in a will, then once the initial grief has passed you will have to invest it. Put it in a high-interest deposit account until you feel able to make a decision rather than rushing into something which could prove to be a mistake in the long term. The BANK, BUILDING SOCIETY and FRIENDLY SOCIETY GUIDES explain the different sorts of account available. It is also worth reading them if you have never had your own account before.

The money you have been left can probably be split into two different groupings. If it was a partner or spouse who died, you may well need the money to live on – at least in the short term until you have your long-term future sorted out. If this is the case then the bulk, if not all, of the money should be invested somewhere low-risk and safe. The guides mentioned in the previous paragraph offer some low-risk solutions. Alternatively, the BOND GUIDE gives details of products that guarantee a fixed level of income or growth and that you will receive your money back. The Government also offers some low-risk investments listed in the NATIONAL SAVINGS GUIDE in the next section.

If you do not need the money immediately then the range of products available widens. The ones mentioned above are still worth looking at, but you may want to widen the range to include shares. The SHARE GUIDE and UNIT TRUST and INVESTMENT TRUST GUIDES explain the different forms of Stockmarket investment, and the PEP GUIDE details a tax-free way of investing. Remember though that equity investment should only be made if you can leave the money in for at least five years.

The same theories apply for any money left to children. The longer it can be left, the more risky the investment can be – if you want. If not, National Savings and many of the building societies and friendly societies offer good investments for children. Before deciding to invest in anything for the long-term, however, see a financial adviser for guidance. The ADVISERS GUIDE in the next section explains the different types of advice available.

Having been through the trauma of a bereavement yourself you will now know the problems that not keeping your affairs in order can cause. While it is not too late for you (and any future partners), make sure you can answer yes to this checklist:

- Have you written and kept up-to-date a will?

- Have you named someone in your will to be guardian of your children, if you have any, should you die while they are still young?

- Have you done as much as possible to reduce any tax that will have to be paid on your estate when you die? See the INHERITANCE TAX and TRUST GUIDES for details.

- Have you taken out adequate life assurance to pay off any debts and provide for your family? See the LIFE ASSURANCE GUIDE if not.

- Does the executor of your will, or some other responsible person, know where all your paperwork, including birth certificate, is kept? Names and addresses of companies providing any life policies, pension arrangements and investments should also be kept in the same place.

If you can answer yes to all these (and don't forget to keep it all up-to-date) then the people you leave behind will be able to sort out your finances easily and quickly and be left to mourn in peace.

## GUIDES MENTIONED IN CHAPTER EIGHT

ADVISERS GUIDE
BANK GUIDE
BOND GUIDE
BUILDING SOCIETY GUIDE
COMPANY PENSION GUIDE
FRIENDLY SOCIETY GUIDE
INHERITANCE TAX GUIDE
INVESTMENT TRUST GUIDE
LIFE ASSURANCE GUIDE
NATIONAL SAVINGS GUIDE
PEP GUIDE
PERSONAL PENSION GUIDE
SHARE GUIDE
TRUST GUIDE
UNIT TRUST GUIDE
WILL GUIDE

# SECTION 2:
# Financial Guides

# ADVISERS GUIDE

BEFORE you take out any financial product, especially the major ones such as a mortgage or pension, you should get professional advice. This comes from people who are trained, and have to pass exams about financial services. They will know which type of product is best suited to your lifestyle and will be able to explain how it works.

There are five main types of financial adviser: direct salespeople; tied agents; insurance brokers; stockbrokers; and independent financial advisers (IFAs) – though some solicitors and accountants will also give financial advice in addition to their main work. None is better than the other – they all perform different roles and it is up to you to decide which type to go and see.

1.   The names and addresses of advisers in your area are listed in the phone book or you can call an insurance company and ask for one of its advisers to come and see you. There is also an organisation called IFA Promotion which will send out a list of three independent advisers in your area if asked (Tel: 0117 971 1177).

**2.** You don't have to want to buy anything specific to go and see a financial adviser – you can just go for a chat and a review of your financial arrangements. The vast majority of advisers work on a commission basis, so the consultation will not cost you anything – but more of that later.

**3.** Only invest your money through registered advisers (the Securities and Investments Board (SIB), the main regulatory body, Tel: 0171 929 3652, will be able to tell you if they are), as they are all members of a compensation scheme. This will pay out if things go wrong and your money is stolen or lost. Details of all the compensation schemes are available from the different regulators and most firms also take part in an ombudsman scheme which will mediate in disputes not covered by the compensation scheme.

**4.** The main types of adviser are:

**Independent financial adviser.** He or she works on your behalf and must scour the market to find the best product for you.

**Direct salespeople.** These women and men work for a life company or investment company – which designs and runs the policies you buy. They can only sell you the range of products sold by the company they work for – but are obliged to tell you if there is not a suitable product in their company's range.

**Tied agent.** This is a person who, while not being a direct employee of a life company (as with the direct salesforce), can only advise on the products of one company. Tied agents normally run their own firm and employ other advisers to work with them.

**Insurance brokers** work in a similar way to independent financial advisers in that they are not tied to one insurance company and must recommend the best products from every single one available on the market. The differences come in the amount of financial services advice the insurance broker gives as part of his or her firm's total and the compensation scheme differs.

**Stockbrokers** are authorised to give advice on buying and selling shares and other related investments such as commodities, gilts and bonds. These are the only people allowed to trade on the Stock Exchange (for which they have to have additional authorisation).

An adviser must tell you how much commission he or she is receiving from the sale of a savings or investment product. As mentioned above, the advice you get is normally 'free' if you do not buy a financial product at the end of it. But if you do then the salesperson will be given part of the money you invest – known as commission. Some advisers do work on a fee basis, however, whereby you pay £50 an hour, for example, regardless of whether you actually buy anything. If you do then buy, the money that the life company would normally pay in commission is invested back into the policy on your behalf.

# ANNUITY GUIDE

IF you have saved during your working life in a pension plan, be it a personal pension or a group scheme, then when you come to retire the chances are you will have to buy your income through an annuity. Only people in a final salary scheme do not need an annuity. See the PERSONAL PENSION GUIDE and COMPANY PENSION GUIDE for further details.

An annuity is simply a way of buying an income for life. This can either be level, rising each year by a fixed amount, or in line with inflation and/or designed to continue paying out to your spouse or partner on your death. The income you receive is based on your age and life expectancy and the current level of interest rates. Once bought, the rate will not change, unless pre-agreed at the outset.

Although we have so far talked about using an annuity to provide an income on retirement, an annuity can be bought at any time and for any reason. The SCHOOL FEES PLANNING GUIDE, INHERITANCE TAX GUIDE and HOME INCOME PLAN GUIDE all give alternative uses for annuities.

But we are going to stick with retirement planning as the example in this guide, as it will be the only time the vast majority of people buy an annuity.

**1.** You have two choices once you have decided to retire – either to use the whole cash lump sum you have built up in your pensions pot to buy an income for the rest of your life, or to take part of the money as a tax-free, cash lump sum and use the remainder to buy an income.

Whichever you choose, the income must be bought via an annuity run by an insurance company or friendly society. Personal pension providers must give you a choice of which company actually provides your annuity – known as an open market option. The annuity is known as a compulsory purchase annuity.

Personal pensions allow you to choose your retirement age from 50 to 75, while company schemes will have different rules depending on the employer. But if you have contracted out of SERPS (the top-up part of the State scheme) this 'protected right', as it is known, must be paid out at age 60 for women and 65 for men regardless of when you actually retire and draw the remainder of the pension.

Remember as well that you can start to receive a personal pension before you actually retire. So you can defer taking out an annuity or stagger it so that the amount increases year by year until you fully retire. This is called staggered vesting and, as with all pension decisions, you should get professional advice before choosing this option. See the ADVISERS GUIDE for the type of advice available.

**2.** When you come to buy the annuity there are a number of different options to choose from. The most common type of annuity is one which pays a fixed, level income for life. But you can also choose one that increases each year. The options for increases range from 3% upwards to linking them to the rate of inflation. The higher you want the escalation each year, the lower the starting income will be.

**3.** You must also choose what other options you want. For example, you can pay for a guarantee providing that, should you die shortly after taking out the annuity, the capital will be repaid, either as a lump sum or as an income for a set number of years, to your spouse or partner. This option will also reduce the level of income you receive.

You can also choose a joint life second death annuity whereby the income will continue until both you and your spouse (or partner if this is allowed) die – rather than the income stopping on your death regardless of how quickly this is after taking out the annuity.

**4.** On the tax side of things the income you receive from an annuity bought with your pension fund is taxable at your highest rate. But if you have a guarantee to repay the unused capital should you die within a certain amount of time then this is paid back tax free, as it is treated as a return of your money by the tax office.

Other types of annuity are treated differently. For example, a purchased life annuity – one which is bought from your own money (other than the pension fund) – is only taxed on part of the income. This is because the Inland Revenue treats part of the income as a repayment of capital (the money you used to buy the annuity in the first place) and part as interest earned on it. The amount you are taxed on is based on the purchase price of the annuity and your life expectancy – the formula is laid down by the Inland Revenue. Since your life expectancy is taken into account, the older you are, the less tax you will have to pay.

The income from an annuity bought by someone else on your behalf, or by you for someone else, is fully income taxable. These include annuities bought in accordance with a will or settlement and ones bought by an employer in recognition of services rendered by an employee (also known as Hancock annuities).

Whichever annuity you buy, make sure the income level you choose will be sufficient for your future needs.

# AVC AND FSAVC GUIDE

AS you approach retirement you may find that you have not paid enough into your company pension – as you have not worked there long enough, for example – to give you an adequate income. But don't despair, there is a way of boosting your pension – either through your employer or on your own – so that you get a healthy income on retirement.

Additional voluntary contribution schemes (AVCs) and free-standing additional voluntary contribution schemes (FSAVCs) are the ways of topping up your company pension. The amount you can pay in each year is limited by the Inland Revenue to 15% of your gross salary. They can also be used to contract out of SERPS (the State Earnings Related Pension Scheme) if your company scheme has not already done so – but this is a complicated process and needs professional advice before being attempted.

Before you read this chapter, read the COMPANY PENSION GUIDE to give you the background on what you are topping up.

**1.** The difference between an AVC and an FSAVC is very simple. An AVC is run by a pension provider alongside your company scheme and you can only pay into this through your company. An FSAVC, meanwhile, can be run by the pension provider of your choice and is not linked to your company scheme. AVCs and FSAVCs are not designed for people with personal pensions.

Many AVCs and all FSAVCs work on what is known as a money purchase basis (like personal pensions). This means that the contributions you pay in build up over the years and the amount of pension you can buy at the end depends on the value of the fund at that time. The alternative, used by a few employers who run final salary schemes, is to use the AVC to 'buy' extra years in the scheme. In this case your final pension is worked out as a percentage of your final salary immediately before or around when you retire. No company pension scheme (with the AVC or FSAVC included) can pay you more than two-thirds of your final salary.

**2.** Once you have started paying into an AVC or FSAVC you cannot take the money out until you retire – as with a normal pension. Remember as well that extra contributions made after 17 March 1987 cannot be used to boost the tax-free, cash lump sum you may receive on retirement. The money must be used to provide an on-going income via an annuity.

# BANK GUIDE

THE first thing to do when choosing a bank account is to decide what you want it to do. Do you just need it as somewhere to deposit money, such as your wages, before you spend it during the month or do you want more from your account? How about an overdraft facility, cheque book, credit card, cash card – with a £50, £100 or £250 limit? Will you save with the bank? Do you want interest paid on the balance?

1. Once you have decided your priorities then it is time to find a bank to provide them. Ask around your friends and family to find out who they bank with and if they are happy with the level of service the bank provides.

    Also find out about the banks in your area. Do their opening times fit in with your lifestyle? Can you get to the bank branches easily?

    Bank services have split in recent years. In addition to the normal bank branches most of the banks also offer telephone banking. While the services they offer are the same as of a regular branch, all transactions and instructions are carried out over the telephone.

Below are the main types of account on offer:

- Current Account/Interest Bearing Current Account
- Cash Card Account
- High Interest Cheque Account
- Instant Access Deposit Account
- Deposit Account
- Instant Access Account
- Notice Account
- Term Account
- Monthly Income Account
- Monthly Savings Account
- Children's Account

On the flip side, banks also offer a range of loan facilities, from authorised (and unauthorised) overdrafts and personal loans to mortgages. This chapter deals only with overdrafts and personal loans; for full details on mortgages, from what they are to how to get one, see the MORTGAGE GUIDE.

## OVERDRAFTS

Most bank accounts – especially those used for day-to-day money management – come with a facility which allows you to borrow money. This is known as an overdraft and should, wherever possible, be arranged in advance. Some bank accounts come with a free overdraft facility which allows you to go into the red without paying any fees, only interest.

The bank sets the amount you can borrow and you only pay interest on the amount that you actually owe, rather than this maximum.

There may well be other arrangement and regular fees to be paid. Overdrafts can be paid back at any time without penalty and most banks will allow you to convert an overdraft into a personal loan if you think you will not be able to repay it quickly. The bank has the right to change the overdraft limit or call in the loan at any time.

An authorised overdraft may sound like it will be expensive to set up, but it pales into insignificance compared with the charges levied if you become overdrawn without asking permission first. This is known as an unauthorised overdraft and will cost about 1% more in interest each month, up to £15 for the letter to tell you that you are overdrawn and around £20 for every cheque that is bounced (not paid by the bank to the person or company you wrote it to). You will also pay much higher monthly or quarterly fees than those charged on an arranged overdraft.

## PERSONAL LOAN

A personal bank loan is a way of borrowing a pre-agreed amount over a fixed period of time. The loan is either secured, backed by your house for example as a second mortgage, which can be taken by the bank if you do not repay the loan, or unsecured. An unsecured loan will cost you more in interest.

Since personal loans are designed to run for a fixed period of time the bank will probably charge a fee if you want to repay the loan early. This currently ranges from the interest to the end of the month to two months' worth.

When you apply for a personal loan, the bank will check that you are creditworthy by looking at your account history and by asking a credit reference agency about you. Credit reference agencies keep detailed information about you, from whether you have any outstanding loans to how regularly you pay your bills on time. If you are turned down for a loan, the bank is not obliged to tell you why, but you can write to the credit reference agencies with £1 for the information they hold about you. If you believe that this is wrong, you can go and see the bank to explain why, and ask for the credit reference agency to change its details.

**2.** You will need several forms of identification ranging from a passport to a recent household bill showing your name and current address to set up an account. If you want interest paid to you gross (without tax) as you are a non-taxpayer, the bank will provide a form for you to fill out.

You are covered by the Bank Savings Compensation Scheme which covers 75% of savings up to £20,000. The maximum compensation is £15,000.

**3.** Once you are comfortable with using a bank account or have decided to save in something other than a savings account, then the bank offers several different tax-free alternatives.

## SAVE AS YOU EARN (SAYE) (SERIES 'F' SHARE OPTION SCHEME)

An SAYE allows you to save regular monthly amounts ranging between £10 and £250 a month for a minimum of five years.

In this type of scheme a company runs an SAYE on behalf of its employees and will give them the option of buying shares at a fixed price (of no less than 80% of the value of the shares when the SAYE was set up) after the five-year period.

After five years the equivalent interest rate is 5.3% tax free (including a bonus of nine months' payments) and employees have the option of buying the shares. Alternatively, if the price of the shares has not risen, has fallen or employees change their mind, the scheme can be kept on for another two years with no more payments made. This boosts the return to 5.87% a year (including a bonus of 18 months' payments). But the entitlement to shares is lost if the scheme is kept open for seven years unless the company running the scheme says otherwise.

## TAX EXEMPT SPECIAL SAVINGS ACCOUNTS (TESSAs)

Set up by the Government in 1991, TESSAs also offer a five-year, tax-free way of saving. Anyone over 18 can set up a TESSA and the maximum savings amount over the five years is £9,000.

This is split up into £3,000 in year one, £1,800 in years two to four and between £600 and £1,800 in year five depending on how much was invested in the first year. There is a maximum monthly saving of £150.

If money is taken out after five years, interest is paid tax free. Withdrawals of capital before then are allowed, but the TESSA's tax-free status will be lost. The equivalent of the net interest payable can be taken without penalty at any time.

All the banks also offer a vast array of other financial products such as building and home contents insurance, life assurance, unit trusts and health insurance. To find out about these different types of insurance look up the individual guides such as HOME INSURANCE GUIDE, UNIT TRUST GUIDE and LIFE ASSURANCE GUIDE.

# BOND GUIDE

BOND is one of the most commonly used terms in the financial services language and, true to form, it can have a variety of different meanings just to keep the average person in the dark.

But bonds aren't complicated – they just appear so. There are two main divisions in the bond world. One set is issued by companies or governments as a way of raising money. The other type, dealt with here, is taken out by you to provide you with either an income or growth of the money you invest (known as capital growth).

The bonds issued by companies or governments (in the UK, Government bonds are also known as gilts) can be bought and sold through a stockbroker (or through the Post Office in the case of gilts) and guarantee to pay a fixed level of income to the holder. The price of the bonds, however, goes up and down, so you could lose money when you sell them if the market is low. If you don't sell them then the company will give you the preset value of the bond, which was decided when it was issued, when it is time for it to repay its debt (ie. when the bond matures). This may be more or less than when you actually paid for it, depending on its market value at the time of purchase.

With most bonds you pay tax on both the income and any growth in your capital. The only exception to the rule is a UK Government gilt. With this, the income is taxed at your normal top rate of 24% or 40% but any capital gains you make are tax free.

All shares and bonds – and any other investments that are 'traded' – work on the basic principle of supply and demand. When more people want to buy than sell the price goes up and when there are more sellers than buyers the price goes down. Sometimes other factors come into play such as the state of the economy or international incidents which also affect the price of your investment. Further details of bonds are given in the SHARE GUIDE.

The other type of bonds – normally called insurance bonds – are designed to give you an income or capital growth over a fixed period. They can be taken out for any length of time, but the longer you are willing to tie up your money the better the return they will give. You cannot trade these types of bond.

1.   Before you take out any type of bond make sure that you can afford to tie up your money for the required period of time. Many of the bonds levy expensive penalties if you want to get your money out early.

Also decide what you want the bond for – income or capital growth or a mixture of both. Ask yourself what level of risk you want to take. Some funds will guarantee a set level of income or growth – but it will be lower than the one you could receive without the guarantee.

2.   Once you have decided that a bond is what you need then it is time to start looking at what is available. Most of the banks and building societies, along with the life companies, offer bonds, so the choice is large. If you can't make up your mind on your own then it is worth getting financial advice. The ADVISERS GUIDE lists the types of advice available.

To help you choose, the main types of bond are listed below.

## BACK TO BACK BOND SCHEMES

With this type of scheme, part of your money is invested in an annuity which pays a guaranteed level of income, while the remainder goes into a single premium insurance bond or a unit trust. The idea is that the annuity provides the income during the bond's life while the unit trust or life fund invested via the insurance bond grows enough to provide you with your capital back at the end.

## GUARANTEED EQUITY BOND

These bonds normally run for five years and guarantee a minimum of your original investment back and a percentage of the rise in the FT-SE 100 Index (which is an index of the 100 biggest companies' shares listed on the Stockmarket). If the FT-SE does not rise over the five years, the capital is still returned, but there is no growth.

## GUARANTEED GROWTH BONDS

Guaranteed growth bonds work exactly as the name suggests. You invest a lump sum of money and after a fixed period of time – normally five years – you are given your money back plus the preset amount of growth. No income is paid on these types of bond.

## GUARANTEED INCOME BONDS

These also work exactly as the name suggests. The bond guarantees to pay a fixed level of income over its life – again normally five years – and return the initial lump sum invested at the end of the period. You will not get any capital growth with this bond.

## HIGH INCOME BONDS

These bonds also run for typically five years. There are no guarantees about the level of income you will receive or that you will actually receive your initial investment back. They do, however, pay a high income which is normally determined by the rise in the FT-SE 100 Index.

## INVESTMENT BONDS

There are insurance bonds linked to certain types of unit trust investment. It is this sort of bond that may be used in the back to back scheme.

## NATIONAL SAVINGS BONDS

Children's Bonus Bond, First Option Bond, Income Bond, Premium Bonds and Pensioner's Guaranteed Income Bond: all these are available via National Savings. For details of how they work see the NATIONAL SAVINGS GUIDE.

## SINGLE PREMIUM BONDS

These are straightforward life assurance bonds. The single premium in the title means that you invest a lump sum rather than small amounts on a regular basis (all the bonds mentioned above require a lump sum investment). The bond invests into a life fund – which is a way of pooling your money with others to buy a wide spread of shares and other investments – thus reducing risk.

## WITH-PROFITS BONDS

These are bonds that invest for a fixed period of time into a with-profits fund. This is one where each year a bonus is paid (called a reversionary bonus) based on the investment growth in the fund throughout the year. At the end of the bond's life a final bonus is paid (called the terminal bonus). This will boost the amount of money you receive back. There are no guarantees and the bond will not pay an income.

# BUILDING SOCIETY GUIDE

THE days of building societies being fuddy-duddy institutions are long gone. Now they are giving the banks a run for their money – and in many cases beating them hands down.

While they are still catching up, the service you get is often better than that of the banks and if you don't have a bank branch near you, there is no reason why you can't do all your normal money management through a building society.

1. Have a look at the building societies in your local area. Many are still regionally based and can offer better rates than the national ones. The flip side to this of course is that they may not be as financially strong (though not in danger of going bust) and could be taken over by a larger society.

**2.**  Before you open anything, ask around your friends and family to see if they bank with a building society and if so what their impression of the service is. While the different accounts on offer will vary slightly in design, all building societies will offer a basic range. We have listed below all the main ones:

- Cheque Book Account

- Cash Card Account

- High Interest Cheque Account

- Instant Access Account

- Ordinary/Share Account

- Postal Account

- Regular Savings Account

- Monthly Income Account

- Notice Account

- Term Share Account

- Children's Account

On the flip side, building societies also offer a range of loan facilities, from authorised (and unauthorised) overdrafts and personal loans to mortgages. This chapter deals only with overdrafts and personal loans. For full details on mortgages, from what they are to how to get one, see the MORTGAGE GUIDE.

## OVERDRAFTS

Some building society accounts – especially those used for day-to-day money management – come with a facility which allows you to borrow money. This is known as an overdraft and should, wherever possible, be arranged in advance. Some building society accounts come with a free overdraft facility, which allows you to go into the red without paying any fees, only interest.

You will often be charged an arrangement fee for setting up an overdraft, plus monthly or quarterly charges, in addition to the interest you must pay on the outstanding loan. The building society sets the amount you can borrow and you only pay interest on the amount that you actually owe, rather than this maximum. Overdrafts can be paid back at any time without penalty and most building societies will allow you to convert an overdraft into a personal loan if you think you will not be able to repay it quickly. The building society has the right to change the overdraft limit, or call in the loan at any time.

An authorised overdraft may sound like it will be expensive to set up, but it pales into insignificance compared with the charges levied if you become overdrawn without asking permission first. This is known as an unauthorised overdraft and will cost about 1% more in interest each month, up to £15 for the letter to tell you that you are overdrawn and around £20 for every cheque that is bounced (not paid by the building society to the person or company you wrote it to). You will also pay much higher monthly or quarterly fees than those charged on an arranged overdraft.

## PERSONAL LOAN

A personal building society loan is a way of borrowing a pre-agreed amount over a fixed period of time. The loan is either secured, backed by your house for example as a second mortgage, which can be taken by the building society if you do not repay the loan, or unsecured. An unsecured loan will cost you more in interest.

Since personal loans are designed to run for a fixed period of time the building society will probably charge a fee if you want to repay the loan early.

When you apply for a personal loan, the building society will check that you are creditworthy by looking at your account history and by asking a credit reference agency about you. Credit reference agencies keep detailed information about you, from whether you have any outstanding loans to how regularly you pay your bills on time. If you are turned down for a loan, the building society is not obliged to tell you why, but you can write to the credit reference agencies with £1 for the information that they hold about you. If you believe that this is wrong, you can go and see the building society to explain why, and ask for the credit reference agency to change its details.

You will need several forms of identification ranging from a passport or driving licence to a recent household bill, showing your name and current address, to open an account. If you want interest paid gross – if you are a non-taxpayer – then the building society will be able to give you the forms to fill out.

**3.** You are covered by the Building Society Savings Compensation Scheme which covers 90% of savings up to £20,000. The maximum payout is £18,000 per person.

**4.** Once you are comfortable with using a building society account or have decided that you would like to save in something other than a savings account, then the building society offers several different tax-free alternatives.

## SAVE AS YOU EARN (SAYE)
## SERIES 'F' SHARE OPTION SCHEME

An SAYE allows you to save regular monthly amounts – ranging from £10 to £250 a month, for a minimum of five years.

In this type of scheme a company runs the SAYE on behalf of its employees and will give them the option of buying shares, at a price fixed at the outset, after the five-year period. The price will be 80% or more of the share price when the SAYE was started. After the five years of saving the yield (interest) is equivalent to 5.3% a year. This is made up of interest plus a bonus equal to nine months' payments. At this point employees have the right to buy shares in the company at the preset price.

Alternatively, if the price of shares has not risen, has fallen or you change your mind, the money can be left in for a further two years – with no more payments made.

This boosts the yield up to 5.87% a year – interest plus a bonus equal to 18 months' payments. But the entitlement to buy shares at the preset price is lost, unless the company running the scheme says otherwise. No partial withdrawals of money can be made and interest is lost if you fully encash the scheme early.

## TAX EXEMPT SPECIAL SAVINGS ACCOUNTS (TESSAs)

Anyone over the age of 18 can set up a TESSA and the maximum that can be saved over the five years is £9,000. This is split up into £3,000 in year one, £1,800 in years two to four and between £600 and £1,800, depending on how much was saved in year one, in year five. A £150 a month maximum saving is also enforced.

If the money is taken out after five years, all the proceeds are tax free. Capital withdrawals during the five years are not allowed – if made the TESSA will lose its tax-free status. But the equivalent of the net interest paid each year can be taken without penalty at any time.

5.   Most of the building societies also offer a vast array of insurance products, usually through a life company owned by the building society or one which it is tied to (see the ADVISERS GUIDE for further details). This basically means that the building society can only sell the products of one company. Not all building societies are 'tied' though, and you should talk to a few before buying anything.

# CAR GUIDE

THERE is only one type of insurance that you legally have to have and this is car insurance – if you have a car, of course.

There are three different types of cover you can buy and which one you choose depends on the value of your car and how much you can afford. These are third party, third party fire and theft, or fully comprehensive. Third party is the legal minimum.

1. Once you buy a car there are three items that you must get before you are allowed to drive it on the road. The first is an MOT proving that the car is roadworthy, the second is car insurance, covering you and other drivers against accidents, and the third is car tax. Driving without these three plus a valid driver's licence is an offence and in very extreme cases could land you in prison.

2. Car insurance covers you against any damage you may do to someone else's car or property and, if you have fully comprehensive cover, the damage to your car as well.

3.     Before you get car insurance it is worth shopping around. Competition is fierce, so the more companies you ring, the better chance there is of finding a good deal.

4.     Find out about the excess on the policy – this is the first part of every claim that you have to pay. The cost of insurance will come down if you are willing to pay more yourself – eg. £200 rather than £100.

5.     Every year you drive without claiming on your insurance helps you build up your no claims bonus. This effectively gives you a discount on the cost of your car insurance. You can also insure this no claims discount – otherwise, when you claim, you risk losing part or all of it and seeing your premiums increase.

6.     If you have an accident with an uninsured driver, there is no insurance company for you to claim from if it was the other driver's fault. To get round this though, the insurance industry has set up a motor claims bureau – run by the Association of British Insurers (ABI) which will pay out if the driver is not covered – but only if you can prove it. If it was a hit and run, for example, then you have no proof that the person was uninsured.

7.     The final thing to remember is that if you take your car abroad to Europe, it is automatically assumed by the authorities in the foreign country that you only have the minimum legal requirement of third party cover. If you have got fully comprehensive cover in the UK then you need to contact your insurer and get the cover extended.

# CARD GUIDE

THERE are various different ways of paying for goods and services these days – cash, cheque, credit cards and a range of other forms of plastic money. This guide explains the different forms of plastic money from credit cards through to budget cards and store cards.

## AUTOMATED TELLER MACHINE (ATM) CARDS

These cards are issued by banks and building societies purely to allow account holders to take money out of cash points (ATMs). The card is linked directly to your account and the money is debited from there, rather than your having to wait for a monthly statement linked to a separate account. To cut down on the amount of cards people have to have, most banks and building societies offer multifunction cards (known as debit cards) which allow money to be taken from a cash point and used instead of a cheque or as a cheque guarantee. To get money from a cash point using any of the different cards available you need a PIN (a Personal Identification Number). This is available from the company that issued the card.

## BUDGET CARDS

Budget cards are a form of credit card, but in this case the credit limit is based on a pre-agreed monthly repayment. The more you can afford to pay back each month as a minimum sum, the higher the credit limit. The cards are mostly issued by retailers as an option on their store cards (see page 109).

## CHARGE CARDS

Charge cards work in a similar way to credit cards in that if you own one you are sent a bill each month. The biggest difference, however, is that you must pay them back in full each month rather than having the option of spreading payments as with a credit card. The benefits of a charge card are that they can be linked to a prearranged overdraft and the issuer of the card may offer priority booking on tickets or free travel insurance for example. They also have no preset spending limit as with credit cards but their annual charges may be higher.

## COMPANY CARDS

These cards, as the name suggests, are offered by employers to some of their staff. Company cards can be either credit or charge cards and are used exactly like the personal versions of these – but the bill is paid by the company.

## CREDIT CARDS

Credit cards are the most common form of card. When you take out a credit card, which usually has an annual fee of £10 or £12, the card issuer will set the credit limit, which is the total amount of money you can owe it from using your card at any one time. Every month a statement (or bill) is sent detailing the minimum amount you must pay back – worked out as a percentage of the total amount you owe. If you do not pay back the debt in full then the outstanding balance (the amount you didn't pay back) is charged interest. The main benefit of owning a credit card is that you can get up to 56 days' interest-free credit.

A variation of the normal credit card is the affinity card, whereby the issuer will make a donation to the charity or organisation that the card is linked to when you open an account. An additional donation is made every time you use the card or when you spend a certain amount.

## DEBIT CARDS

Debit cards have three uses: they act as a cheque guarantee card, guaranteeing payment up to their set limit – normally £50 or £100; as an alternative to a cheque – whereby the card is used like a credit card but the money is debited directly from the account, rather than a separate bill received each month; and as a cash point card which allows you to take money from one of the automated teller machines (ATMs).

## GOLD CARDS

Gold cards are an elevated form of credit or charge card. Issuers offer them to their often high-earning (and spending) customers. They normally have a higher credit limit than the normal credit or charge card equivalent and the annual charges rise correspondingly. The benefits they offer include overdrafts at a preferential rate, priority booking with many airlines and insurance to cover major purchases.

## STORE CARDS

Store cards can take three different forms: either a charge card, budget card or credit card. The interest rate charged on these cards is often higher than that of a credit card, and they can only be used in the shop or group of shops issuing the card.

**1.** Listed in this chapter are the main types of plastic card available. Some are easier to get than others, for example; half the people who apply for a credit card are turned down as their credit rating is not good enough; but none is compulsory.

Credit rating is used by both card companies and other financial services groups such as banks and building societies to determine whether you are a good credit risk – basically whether you can afford and are likely to pay back any money owed when it is due.

All the organisations have their own versions of credit scoring or use an outside credit reference agency. If you are turned down for credit, the company is not legally required to tell you why, though you can write to a credit reference agency enclosing £1 to find out what details it keeps about your credit record.

**2.** Under the Consumer Credit Act of 1974, you are automatically protected against damaged or faulty goods or their not turning up, if you bought them with your credit card. But *each* item must have cost between £100 and £30,000 – not the total transaction. Debit cards (except the Lloyds debit card) and charge cards are not covered by the Consumer Credit Act.

# COMPANY PENSION GUIDE

YOUR retirement years have the potential to be the best years of your life. Finally, you are free of work and with a bit of planning beforehand should have money to spend doing the things that you want to do, not have to do.

To plan for your retirement you can save money into a pension. This, unlike other types of saving scheme such as a personal equity plan (PEP), is designed especially to provide you with an income when you stop work. As an incentive the Government gives you tax relief on the money you put in and lets the funds grow free of tax. But once in, you cannot touch the money – except to move it between different pension schemes – until you retire.

Pension schemes can be roughly divided into two – personal pension plans and company pension schemes – though there will be variations in the exact running of these two types. This chapter deals with company schemes, and for further details of personal pensions see the PERSONAL PENSION GUIDE further on in this section.

Briefly, the basic difference between company and personal pensions is that a company scheme is run by your employer and you may pay into it only while you work for the company, whereas a personal pension belongs to you and can be taken from job to job. You can only pay into one of the different types of pension at any one time – except in set circumstances.

One such instance is if your company scheme is not 'contracted out' you can use a personal pension or AVC (see the AVC AND FSAVC GUIDE) to contract out of SERPS. This is the 'extra part' of the State pension which is linked to the amount of years you have worked and is based on one-fifth of your lifetime earnings. If you contract out, the Government will give you the money that has accumulated over the years you have worked plus a little bit extra (about 1% if you are over 30) to put into your own pension plan (be it a personal or company scheme). The State will also continue to pay in the amount that would have been the SERPS element of your State pension each year. If you are a member of a company scheme which you contract out of, you cannot put extra money (above the SERPS payment) into the personal pension.

The State pension is made up of two parts – the basic amount which everyone will receive, provided they have paid enough National Insurance contributions, and the SERPS element. Self-employed people do not qualify for SERPS, so cannot contract out of it. Get professional advice before you contract out of SERPS, as it is not a good idea for everybody. You can find out how much SERPS rights you have built up so far, and what your payments would be if you stayed in it until you retire, by filling in the application form in the leaflet *Your Future Pension* (leaflet NP38 available from your local Social Security office).

If you do choose to contract out of SERPS then the money given to you by the State becomes the 'protected rights' part of your pension. Some company schemes are already contracted out – so you cannot do this yourself as well. If your scheme is contracted out, but you would be better off contracted in, it may be possible to do this while staying in your employer's scheme. Talk to the pension trustees – the people who run the pension fund on the employer's and your behalf – to see whether this is possible.

You can only pay into a pension if you are earning. And you can be earning anything from a full-time job to answering the telephone for your partner's business and doing a bit of typing in your spare time. Don't worry if you don't earn enough to pay tax or National Insurance; you can still take out your own pension – and get tax relief on the contributions (ie. the money you pay in).

**1.** You can only join the company pension scheme of the firm you work for. Once you leave you have to stop paying into the scheme and become a member of your new employer's one if there is one. Joining a company scheme will not stop your getting a State pension, provided you have paid enough National Insurance stamps.

Once you leave a company you have two choices – either to leave the money in the scheme and let it grow until you are ready to retire, or take it with you and put it into your new company's pension scheme or a personal pension. But get professional financial advice before doing anything with your money or you may lose out when you come to take the pension. The ADVISERS GUIDE in this section explains the different types of advice available. If you leave a company scheme within two years of joining it, however, the trustees who run the pension fund do not have to give you a pension when you retire. The most likely route in this case is that you will get a refund of the premiums you have put in less tax – but not the money put in on your behalf by your employer. This is the only time you can get the money put aside for a pension before you retire.

**2.** There are three main types of company pension scheme: final salary, money purchase and group personal pension scheme. Which one is offered is decided by your employer. You do not have to join the pension scheme run by your employer and you can leave it, once in, without having to leave the company itself.

The most popular type of company pension is a *final salary* or *final pay scheme*. With this type of scheme the pension you receive is based on your salary on or near to retirement and the number of years you have been a member of the scheme. The maximum you can receive is two-thirds of your final salary.

A *money purchase scheme* works like a personal pension in that the amount of money you have on retirement depends on how much you (and your employer) have put in and how much the money has grown by (known as the investment return or rate). The more you put in and the better it grows, the more money you will have to buy an annuity – a guaranteed income for life.

Some employers run a hybrid version of the two schemes mentioned above. For example, the basic scheme may be dependent on the investment performance of the fund but you are also guaranteed not to get less than a certain percentage of your salary times the number of years you have been in the scheme.

*Group personal pensions* work in exactly the same way as a personal pension except that you and your workmates all have your plans run by a single pension provider. Doing it this way means that the amount each person receives is based on his or her contributions and the rate of growth in the fund, but the charges may well be lower than each of you taking out your own individual personal pension.

**3.** Nine times out of ten a company pension scheme will offer a better deal for you than a personal pension. But there will be occasions when you are better off taking out a personal pension or moving your money from a company pension to a personal one. This is known as a transfer, and the transfer value is worked out for you by a professional, normally within the pension scheme.

4. As with a personal pension, tax relief is paid at your highest rate – and your employer also gets tax relief on the contributions he or she makes on your behalf.

5. The final two pension schemes worth mentioning are designed for top executives (executive pension plans) and for small family businesses (small self-administered schemes).

*Executive pension plans* are designed for senior employees and controlling directors. They allow the scheme members to invest several times more each year than their actual salary. But since they are written as a final salary scheme under the company pension rules the two-thirds of salary rule applies – the maximum you can actually receive under any final salary scheme. The idea is that, as a high-flying executive, you will be earning so much by the time you retire that you have to start overpaying into your pension now to actually reach those limits by the time you give up work.

A *small self-administered scheme* is also run by an insurance or pension company on the member's behalf, but unlike an executive pension the members choose where the money is invested – be it stocks and shares, property or other assets. The vast majority of SSASs, as they are known, have less than 12 members, making them ideal for small, family-run firms or the top executives of a larger firm. The only potential difficulty is that most schemes require all the members of an SSAS to be trustees and total agreement from all trustees is needed before the money can be invested in anything.

# CRITICAL ILLNESS INSURANCE GUIDE

THE sad fact is that almost all of us are likely to suffer from a critical condition at some point in our lives. We have a one in three chance of contracting cancer and 150,000 people suffer a heart attack each year with a further 100,000 having a stroke.

While no financial product can stop our suffering the illness itself, critical illness insurance can stop our suffering financial hardship during this time.

1.  Once you have decided that you need cover, the first thing to do is to choose the type of cover you need. Do you want it to stand on its own and not cover any particular loan – stand alone, or linked to your mortgage – a mortgage endowment policy with critical illness attached? Also decide how long you want cover for. There are two options: either a whole of life policy – which covers you until death, or a fixed-term product – running for 20 years, for

example. Check the small print though, as some companies stop the cover after age 65 or 70.

2.    Next decide whether you want death benefits attached – this means the policy will pay out on diagnosis of any of the critical conditions, or on death if you do not claim beforehand. The good thing about having death benefits attached is that it means your surviving partner or family will get a cash payout if you do not contract a critical condition.

The drawback is that if you do claim during your lifetime you are left without life cover on death, which could put your family in financial difficulties. Alternatively, if you receive a cash payout and die shortly after, you will leave a cash-rich estate. This means there will be unforeseen inheritance tax liabilities. One way round this is to write the policy in trust (see the TRUST GUIDE). On balance it is probably better to separate the two – though speak to your financial adviser before signing anything. See the ADVISERS GUIDE for different types of advice available.

3.    Next decide how much cover you want – or can afford. The policy will pay out after about 30 days from diagnosis of the range of critical conditions you have chosen. Remember it is not designed for non-serious diseases such as minor skin cancers or flu. Make sure that you read the small print and know what is excluded – which is equally as important as what is included – before you sign. If you don't understand anything, ask your adviser – he or she is there to help.

# FRIENDLY SOCIETY GUIDE

FRIENDLY societies have been around a long time. They were originally set up by groups of like-minded people – such as miners or nurses – to provide for each other when one fell sick or was involved in an accident and unable to work. They reached the height of their popularity in about 1908 and have been losing ground ever since. The sharp decline in their popularity came about with the creation of the Welfare State which was also designed to take care of people when they were unable to work.

But friendly societies, after years of wallowing in the doldrums, are on the up again. The Friendly Societies Act 1992 opens the way for them to offer the full range of financial services including unit trusts, personal equity plans (PEPs) and general insurance such as motor and household cover.

The vast majority of the 457 friendly societies, however, will be closed to the average person, as they are specifically designed to provide investment, sickness benefits and sometimes pensions to a particular group of people – such as civil servants through the Civil Servant Annuities Assurance Society. But some are open to the general public and currently offer several useful policies:

1. The best known is the friendly society tax-exempt bond. This allows you to invest up to £200 a year (£18 a month) or invest a lump sum (of around £2,000 depending on the society) into a linked account which drip feeds the money in over the term (as if you were only investing a little each month or year). In return you get life cover should you die during the investment period – which is ten years – plus a tax-free return when it matures.

The money itself is invested in either a unit-linked fund – which pools your money with other people's and invests it in a wide range of shares, thus reducing the risk of losing all your money in one go – or a with-profits fund. A with-profits fund again puts your money in a big pot, but each year a bonus is paid (called a reversionary bonus) which once given cannot be taken away. At the end of the bond's life a final bonus is given (called the terminal bonus) which boosts the return you receive. The value of a unit-linked fund goes up and down over the life of the bond depending on how well the investments are performing, and nothing is guaranteed.

Because the total amount you can invest in the bond is small – only £2,000 over ten years – many parents or grandparents use it to provide savings for their children or grandchildren.

2. The other policy friendly societies are well known for is the Permanent Health Insurance plan (PHI). This plan is designed to pay out an income if you are unable to work due to sickness or injury. Although the cost may be more expensive in the early years, as you get older the premiums stay low compared to other PHI plans. See

the PERMANENT HEALTH INSURANCE GUIDE for further details. You will also get a cash lump sum at the end of the policy's life – normally when you reach age 60 or 65. The cut-off date is set at this age as PHI is designed to replace wages if you are unable to work, rather than a pension once you retire.

3.  The final main friendly society product is a pension. This works the same way as a normal pension in that you pay money in each month or year and when you retire, this pot of money – plus any growth in the capital and income that has been reinvested while it was not needed – is used to provide you with an income on retirement. See the PERSONAL PENSION GUIDE for further details.

4.  As the friendly societies start to implement the changes introduced in the Friendly Societies Act 1992, their product range will grow. As it does, they will gradually move back into the mainstream and eventually become household names – like their building society, bank and life company rivals.

# HOME INCOME PLAN GUIDE

THERE are a lot of elderly people who do not have enough money, from their pension or other sources, to live, but do have tens of thousands of pounds locked up in the bricks and mortar of the home they live in.

If you are in this situation or have a sneaky suspicion that you may find yourself in it because of inadequate pension provisions, don't panic – there is a way round this poverty trap. The way out is through a home income plan. This is a way of unlocking the capital in your home while still living in it until you are ready to move.

1. There are three main types of home income plan:

## HOME INCOME SCHEMES
Under these types of scheme a mortgage loan is taken out against the value of the property. The proceeds are then used to buy a purchased

life annuity, which pays out a preset amount of income monthly or annually.

This income is used to pay off the interest on the loan and provide you with a regular income. The interest rate you pay on the loan is normally fixed at the outset and a cash lump sum of up to 10%, normally £3,000 maximum, of the loan can be taken immediately.

This money can be used to pay off other debts or for home improvements or for anything you want.

Once you or your spouse, if the annuity is written on a joint life last survivor basis (see the ANNUITY GUIDE), dies then the house is sold and used to repay the loan. Any money left over is paid into your estate for your beneficiaries (the people your money and possessions were left to in your will). See the WILL GUIDE for details of writing a will.

## HOME REVERSION SCHEMES

These schemes allow you to sell a percentage of your property, usually between 40% and 100%. The amount you receive in the form of a guaranteed income for life is based on the value of your property. The reversionary company will pay between 30% and 60% of the value of the property and the younger you are, the less you will get. This is because the company has longer to wait until it can take vacant possession and sell the property to realise its loan and get its money back.

The guaranteed income is paid via an annuity or based on the value of the company's property fund. This is made up of all the properties the company has bought and the income comes from the sale of the houses as and when people die or wish to move.

## EQUITY RELEASE MORTGAGE SCHEMES

This type of scheme can be divided into two: the first is a mortgage loan (usually from a building society) with interest payable. The other is a loan where the interest is rolled up over the life of the loan and is repayable either on death or when the loan reaches a certain percentage of the value of the house.

The money released by the loan can be invested anywhere you like, used to make home improvements or whatever you want to do with it. If you do choose this type of scheme, make sure you invest the money wisely or you could find yourself worse off than you were before. Overall equity release mortgage schemes are NOT to be recommended.

There are also various hybrid schemes available which allow you to sell off your house in tranches, for example, and buy different length annuities (ie. five years) with the proceeds, or fit the amount of income you require.

**2.** Getting good financial advice is imperative before taking out a home income plan. Five companies which offer the home income and home reversion schemes have set up a group called the Safe Home Income Plan (SHIP) group. The companies are: Hinton & Wild, Allchurches Life, Carlyle Life, Home and Capital Trust and Stalwart Assurance. All follow a code of practice and further details can be obtained from Hinton & Wild (Tel: 0181 390 8166).

**3.** Make sure you understand exactly what you are committing yourself to before you sign anything, and always tell your children or any close family and friends what you are doing.

# HOME INSURANCE GUIDE

ONCE you have found the house or flat you want to live in, it is vital that you insure the building and your possessions within it. Unlike a car though, insurance is not compulsory.

There are two types of insurance for the home – buildings insurance and home contents. If you are renting a flat, the buildings insurance will normally be paid for by your landlord, either through the rent you pay each month or through the ground rent/service charge.

If you own your own home, one of the conditions of getting the mortgage will have been that you take out buildings insurance – either through your lender or another insurance company. Many lenders will offer deals with lower interest rates in return for your taking out their buildings insurance and/or contents insurance.

Buildings insurance covers you for the cost of rebuilding your home if it is damaged through a fire or flood, for example. The cover is normally index-linked, rising in line with the house building index, to stop there being a shortfall should any work need to be done.

The other insurance – home contents – can be linked to the buildings insurance or taken out as a separate policy. Home contents cover will pay out the cost of replacing your possessions, from the TV through to new china to the bed covers, should they be stolen or damaged.

1. The first thing to do when you move into your new home is to decide the value of the contents within it. The best way to do this is to go through, room by room, totalling up the cost of replacing all the items. Some things will, of course, be irreplaceable – because they have sentimental value, for example – but you should still have the money available to replace them with something else.

2. Once you have worked out the value of the contents in your home – and don't forget the carpets and curtains in this – then it is time to find the right sort of cover for you. Remember that if you under-insure yourself, when you come to make a claim the insurance company can scale the claim down, or even refuse to pay out anything as you have lied, called 'non-disclosure', by underestimating the value of your possessions.

3. There are four main types of home contents insurance policy and it is worth shopping around for the one that best suits your needs.

   The first is *indemnity cover*. With this policy you tell the insurer how much cover you want. When you come to make a claim this is what you are paid out, less a little for wear and tear on the items (depending on their ages). You therefore get the value of the item when it was stolen or broken – regardless of what it will cost to replace at current prices.

The more common type of cover these days is *new-for-old insurance*. Like indemnity cover you tell the insurer the amount you wish to insure. But when you come to make the claim, you are covered for the amount it will actually cost to replace the item, such as a TV, in real terms, regardless of what it cost in the first place. The only exception to this is that linens and items such as bicycles will have an amount deducted from them for wear and tear.

The third main type of cover is a *bedroom rated policy*. With this the insurer sets the amount of cover you get based on the number of bedrooms in your house. For example, your insurer may decide that houses with three bedrooms need £20,000 worth of cover.

The final, and newest, type of insurance is an *unlimited policy*. With this the insurer sets the rate and there is no maximum sum assured, though there are limits on the amounts that can be claimed for individual items.

**4.** Make sure you keep both the buildings and home contents cover up to date. Allow for inflation and prices rising above this when you renew your cover each year. The last thing you want is to have to pay to replace goods in your house after the trauma of a burglary or fire because you were underinsured.

# INHERITANCE TAX GUIDE

SADLY, you can't escape paying taxes, even in death. But you can make it more difficult for the tax office to get its hands on most of your hard-earned possessions.

Inheritance tax (known as IHT) affects one estate in 25 – about 22,000 individuals each year – and raises £1.25 billion annually for the Treasury. But it is also known as the 'voluntary tax', as there are many ways of planning your affairs legally to avoid paying it.

If you haven't written a will yet, do this first, but bear in mind the effects of your gifts in terms of the tax that will have to be paid once you die, by both the estate (this is how all your possessions are known once you die) and any tax your beneficiaries will have to pay on gifts you leave them – such as capital gains tax. To help, see the WILL GUIDE further on in the section for guidelines on how to write a will and the effects of dying without one.

Inheritance tax is payable on the value of an estate above £200,000

(1996/7 tax year) – below this no tax is payable. If you do have to pay it, IHT is charged at 40% – though gifts given up to seven years before death have a reduced scale of tax (see below). The bulk of inheritance tax owing must be paid before the estate can be paid out to the beneficiaries. But tax owing on assets such as a house, land or business can be delayed for up to ten years.

There are, however, some basic exemptions to inheritance tax shown below. The annual gifts can be given each tax year – 6 April to 5 April:

- *Spouse exemption:* Anything left by you to your spouse, or vice versa, is inheritance tax free.

- *Annual exemption:* Gifts of up to £3,000 a year can be given away free of inheritance tax. Unused portions can be brought forward one year.

- *Marriage gifts exemption:* Money given as a wedding present. Parents – £5,000 each; grandparents, great-grandparents, the bride and groom to each other – £2,500; anyone else – £1,000.

- *Small gifts exemption:* As many individual gifts of £250 as desired can be made each year to anyone, provided they have not received money from either of the two options above.

- *Normal gifts from income:* As much as you like can be given as a gift, free of inheritance tax, on a regular basis – provided it comes out of your normal income and does not reduce your standard of living. You must be able to prove that the money was given regularly (or if a person dies suddenly, intended to be given regularly) to avoid paying tax on it.

- *Lifetime gifts:* These are exempt from inheritance tax if the money is to be used to provide for the upbringing of children or a dependent relative.

- *Other exemptions:* Gifts and bequests to a range of organisations and purposes are also IHT free. These organisations are: charities, political parties and universities. Also exempt are gifts for national purposes or public benefit.

There are also a number of tax reliefs on transfers, made either during your lifetime or on death, on businesses and agricultural land.

1. First, sit down and estimate what you are worth. This does not have to be accurate to the last penny, as the value of the estate will change in time with inflation and interest earned on any investments or savings. Remember, if you live in a home that you don't own but retain the right to live in during your lifetime, then it will be taken as part of your estate for inheritance tax purposes. A lifetime interest is something, ie. a house, which is held in trust for someone else but you have the right to use – or if it is shares, the income produced by them – until you die. You are not, however, allowed to sell or spend any of the capital.

2. Once you have decided how much you are worth then you must decide how much you want to leave and to whom. Make sure that your will is up to date and that the people and amounts that you want to leave to each person are listed in it.

3. Wherever possible use the exemptions listed above. Since transfers between spouses are IHT free, it is worth splitting all your possessions down the middle. This way, when you die, only half your estate will be liable to IHT – each spouse has his or her own £200,000 IHT limit.

With a house there are two types of joint ownership. The most common is a joint tenancy. This means if one partner dies then the other is automatically entitled to his or her half, regardless of what the will says. The other is a house owned through a tenants-in-common agreement. This allows your share of the property to form part of your estate and be left to anyone you wish. A word of caution though: if you do decide to follow the tenants-in-common route, make sure that your will clearly states that your spouse or partner has a life interest in the property and cannot be forced to move and the house sold unless he or she agrees.

**4.** The other thing to do – if you can afford it – is to give gifts, written in trust for future generations such as children or grandchildren. These fall outside the inheritance tax exemptions listed above but do become IHT free if you survive for more than seven years. Trusts have many uses in inheritance tax planning, but outside this they also allow you to leave money to whomever you want, for them to receive it when you say so – eg. when a child reaches 18 or 21 – and put conditions on a person receiving the money.

These gifts are known as potentially exempt transfers (PETs) and they are subject to a reduced rate of tax if you survive more than three years but less than seven from making them. Unfortunately, though, if the gift is made less than seven years beforehand, the Inland Revenue will normally treat it as part of the £200,000 exempt value (if less than this) of the estate and charge the full 40% on the total of the remainder, rather than letting you pay a reduced tax rate on the lifetime gift in addition to your £200,000 exemption.

The tax bands are:

| | | |
|---|---|---|
| Between one and three years | = | 40% tax on 100% of the gift |
| Between three and four years | = | 40% tax on 80% of the gift |
| Between four and five years | = | 40% tax on 60% of the gift |
| Between five and six years | = | 40% tax on 40% of the gift |
| Between six and seven years | = | 40% tax on 20% of the gift |
| Over seven years | = | no tax to pay |

There are several other types of PET that can be set up to provide for your family or friends: the gift mentioned above; an accumulation and maintenance trust (whereby all the beneficiaries must be under 25 when the trust is set up and at least one must receive the money by the age of 25); and a trust where the beneficiary has the right to all the income. All these are subject to the tax rates listed above. How to set up the trusts themselves is explained more fully in the TRUST GUIDE, but it is vital to get additional financial (and often legal) advice before acting. See the ADVISERS GUIDE for different types of financial advice.

If a gift with reservation is made, however, then the full 40% of inheritance tax is payable. An example of a gift with reservation is gifting a house to a relative or friend but retaining a right to live in it until you die – the only exemption is if you pay the full market rent each month to the new 'owners'.

**5.** Life policies can also be used to reduce the effects of inheritance tax or pay off any tax liability. Since IHT has to be paid before an estate can be paid out to the named beneficiaries, it makes sense to ensure that there is enough cash around – preferably outside the estate – to pay it.

The most common life product used for inheritance tax planning is a whole of life policy written in trust – which puts it outside your estate on death and means it is both exempt from an inheritance tax liability and can be easily accessed. This is taken out for the estimated amount of your inheritance tax liability. See the LIFE ASSURANCE GUIDE for details of the different types and ways life policies work.

If you are married and intend to leave all your possessions to your spouse (and vice versa), then the policy should be written as a joint life second death policy, so tax is paid on the second death when the estate goes to friends or family.

As mentioned earlier, if you have made an outright gift to someone, you must live for seven years after giving the gift to make it IHT free. To shield the estate and the beneficiary from the effect of inheritance tax should you die within seven years, term assurance can be taken out to cover the amount of tax that would be payable during the period on the gift.

**6.** If you do want to give a gift, but need the income or capital to live on, then the life insurance industry has devised various schemes to help you get round this problem.

The three main ones are back to back schemes, retained interest schemes, and discounted gift schemes, though you could also use a gift and loan scheme. A financial adviser or solicitor/accountant should be able to explain these schemes in detail and recommend the most appropriate one for your circumstances.

# INVESTMENT TRUST GUIDE

MUCH the safest way to invest in the Stockmarket is to pool your money with other people and use the total kitty to invest in a wide spread of shares.

This can be done in two ways: through an investment trust or a unit trust. While the overall effect is the same – you will receive either income, capital or a mixture of both – the way each type of trust achieves it is somewhat different. (See the UNIT TRUST GUIDE for further details of these trusts.)

Remember, though, both these types of savings are for the long term. If you will need the money within five years then look at one of the other types of investment. See the BOND GUIDE or NATIONAL SAVINGS GUIDE for ideas.

Investment trusts can be used for a variety of things – paying off a mortgage, long-term savings, to pay school fees or just saving up for some luxury like an exotic holiday.

1.  The first step is to decide whether an investment trust is right for you. Ask yourself a few questions: What do I want the money for? When will I need it? How much can I afford to save?

    You can save via an investment trust in two ways. Either a one-off lump sum investment or by saving regular small amounts each month through an Investment Trust Saving Scheme (ITSS). A list of companies that run these regular savings schemes is available from the Association of Investment Trust Companies (AITC) (Tel: 0171 432 5222).

2.  Then decide what you want your savings to do for you: provide a regular income or capital growth.

    Investment trusts can be roughly split into two groupings: those that provide a regular – and hopefully – growing income and those that provide capital growth. With the income trusts, the dividends, as the income payments are known, can be reinvested to boost the small amount of capital growth you'll get, if you don't need them immediately. Or, on the flip side, most capital growth trusts will provide a small amount of income – which can also be reinvested.

In the middle of these two are balanced investment trusts. These trusts place equal emphasis on income and growth in your capital (your initial investment) – though neither will be as great as investing in a trust that invests specifically for one or the other.

There are also investment trusts that allow you to choose either an income share or a capital share – within the same trust. They are known as split capital investment trusts and are explained in greater detail further on in this chapter.

Investment trusts, unlike unit trusts, can borrow money to boost their returns to investors. Known as gearing, the loan is backed by the shares the investment trust holds (as the mortgage loan you have is given against your house) and the lenders have first call on the money if the interest or capital is not repaid as promised (in the same way your house can be repossessed if you don't pay off the mortgage each month).

Unlike normal companies such as ICI, investment trusts do not actually produce anything. All they do is invest in the shares of other companies.

The practical effect of this is that the shares of investment trusts do not reflect the value of the underlying portfolio of shares a manager has bought. The true value of the portfolio is known as the Net Asset Value (NAV) – and the shares in the trust can be bought at a discount, or premium, to the actual value of the NAV.

For example, an investment trust trading at an 8% discount would allow you to buy £100 worth of assests for just £92. At the other end of the scale, an investment trust trading at an 8% premium means that you would pay £108 for £100 worth of assets.

3. There are some investment trusts that cannot be categorised neatly as either income, capital growth or balanced trusts. These are known as split capital investment trusts.

The simplest split capital investment trusts have just two classes of share: one for income – the income share, and the other for capital growth – the capital share. Split capital trusts have a fixed life – normally eight to ten years. Some of the newer investment trusts are more complicated.

## INCOME SHARES

There are three different types of income share: traditional income shares as mentioned above which get all income plus their money back (the initial cost at launch), plus sometimes a little more on wind-up; income shares that receive all the income during the trust's life but have no or a nominal entitlement to capital, ie. 1p per share at wind-up (these are often known as annuity income shares); and those that are entitled to income during the trust's life and any capital left over after other classes of share (such as zero dividend preference shares – see below) have been paid.

## CAPITAL SHARES

These shares do not receive any income during the trust's life but are entitled to capital after the income and preference shareholders have been paid out.

## ZERO DIVIDEND PREFERENCE SHARES

Like capital shares, zeros are not entitled to any income during the trust's life. But unlike capital shares, they have a preset capital return when the trust is wound up and take precedence over all other classes of split capital share.

## STEPPED PREFERENCE SHARES

Stepped preference shares are similar to zeros in that they have a fixed capital return at the end of the trust's life. But they differ in that they are also entitled to a fixed and rising level of income (hence their name).

## HIGHLY GEARED ORDINARY SHARES/ORDINARY SHARES

These shares are entitled to all the income during a trust's life plus any capital left over after other classes of share have been paid out. Ordinary shares (or highly geared ordinary shares as they are often known) are normally coupled with zeros and will get the capital growth left over when this class of shareholder has been paid out.

## WARRANTS

Some investment trusts, both split level and traditional (single share class) ones, offer warrants attached to the shares. Initially offered when the trust is launched, they entitle a person to, for example, one share at the issue price for every five bought. Both the price of the share and how long the offer is for (eg. four or five years) is known at the outset and the warrants can be bought and sold just like the shares themselves.

With all the different types of split capital share mentioned above, there are various rules of thumb that need to be used before you buy. The Association of Investment Trust Companies (AITC) produces a series of measurements that can be used to work out whether there is enough value in the portfolio to repay each shareholder when the trust is wound up.

**4.**  Once you have decided how much you can afford to invest and what type of share (or shares) you want to invest in, then it is time to decide on the trust. The rule here is the more you narrow the investment field, the more risky the fund will be. For example, a fund investing in hi-tech companies in India will be more volatile than one investing in large, blue-chip companies across the world.

**5.**  If you know which trust you want, you can either go directly to the fund management company that runs the trust or via an intermediary – either a financial adviser or stockbroker. If you have not decided what trust you want to invest in, then an adviser will be able to guide you (see the ADVISERS GUIDE in this section).

# LIFE ASSURANCE GUIDE

If you have people who depend on you, then taking out life assurance is a must. The emotional trauma will be bad enough for them if you die; they shouldn't have to worry about money as well.

There are various different types of life assurance available – ranging from ones that last just a few years to others that can be taken out for the whole of your life. Each serves a different function – the shorter ones to cover a specific loan, for example, or while your children are young, and others that can be used both to provide cover – and some investment if you want – throughout your life, and help pay any inheritance tax on your death.

Life cover can be bought direct from an insurance company or, if you are not quite sure which type you need, through a financial adviser. The ADVISERS GUIDE explains the different types of advice available. This chapter lists the main types of life cover you can buy and the pros and cons of each.

143

Although there are many forms of life assurance there is a common thread that runs through them all. In each, you decide how much cover you want and the premiums are then worked out according to your age, sex, state of health and lifestyle. Most of them will also allow you to choose how and when the policy pays out. This means that you can just insure yourself, or take out a joint policy with your spouse or partner, with the money being paid out on either the first or second death, as you wish.

With all types, you also have the option of nominating who you want to receive the money – be it your spouse or the bank that lent you the money to buy your new car. Life assurance can, and normally should, be written in trust. This means that if you die the money does not form part of your estate (as your possessions are known once you die) and thus can be got at immediately, even if your will has not yet been read and the estate distributed in accordance with your wishes. For further information on trusts see the TRUST GUIDE later in this section.

Finally, most life assurance policies give you the option of taking out what is called waiver of premium cover. This allows you to stop paying the premiums if you are unable to work through sickness, injury or unemployment.

## TERM ASSURANCE

This is the cheapest form of life cover you can buy. It is designed to run for any period of time – from literally a month to 20 or 30 years or more. You choose the amount you want paid out on your death – known as the sum assured – and the premiums are worked out from this. If you die during the period of insurance, your family or whomever you have named as the beneficiary will receive this money.

*Basic level term assurance* gives you a fixed amount of cover. Both the premiums and sum assured are preset at the outset and cannot be changed during the policy's life. If you survive the term of the policy then you will not get any money back.

*Increasing term assurance* lets you increase the sum assured each year. You can choose the amount of increase at outset, say 5% a year, or have it go up in line with inflation. The premiums will also go up each year to take account of the increased sum assured.

*Decreasing term assurance* allows you to reduce the amount of life cover you have over the life of the policy. As the level of cover falls, so do the premiums.

*Convertible term assurance* gives you the option of switching from term assurance into a different type of policy such as whole of life cover at any time during the policy's life.

*Family income benefit.* This type of term assurance will pay out a fixed amount of income over a set period of time after you die. It is another form of decreasing term assurance in that the amount of money the person you name as the beneficiary gets, falls year by year over the fixed period of time.

*Pension term.* This is a level term assurance cover but set up inside your pension. Because the policy is moulded into a pension the premiums you pay attract tax relief at your highest amount. The amount of cover is limited though. The Inland Revenue will only allow 5% of your net wages (wages after tax) to be used to buy life cover if you have a personal pension, and within a company scheme the benefits (the money paid out on your death) must not be more than four times your salary. See the COMPANY PENSION GUIDE and the PERSONAL PENSION GUIDE for further details.

## ENDOWMENT ASSURANCE

The next two types of life assurance both have investment elements to them, which means that if you survive the term of the policy you will receive some money back.

*Endowments* are best known as a method of paying off a mortgage (see the MORTGAGE GUIDE), but they can be used for any purpose you like. You can choose any period of cover, starting normally from ten years.

Endowments, and whole of life policies, have two ways of investing: through a unit-linked fund or a with-profits one.

A *with-profits fund* is a way of investing in a range of shares, fixed interest securities such as gilts and even property, but without the volatility (whereby the price of the investment goes up and down) of a unit-linked fund.

Your money is pooled in the with-profits fund and every year a bonus is allocated to all investors (called the reversionary bonus), with the amount depending on how well the fund has performed throughout the year. Once given, this bonus cannot be taken away, regardless of the performance of the fund in future years. At the end of the policy's life a final bonus (known as the terminal bonus) is paid, which can boost the return you receive by as much as 50%. The idea is that since the growth of the fund relies on the addition of bonuses it will grow smoothly throughout the term and thus provide a low-risk option.

A *unit-linked fund* has a much closer link with the underlying portfolio – the shares and other types of investment the pot of money (known as the life fund) has bought. Because of this, the value of the fund goes up and down day by day and there are no guarantees of the minimum you will receive back when the policy matures. With a with-profits fund you will always get back at least the value of your fund at the last bonus payment date.

Some companies also offer a unit-linked fund which acts like a with-profits policy. This is called a *unitised with-profits fund* and will be offered alongside the company's range of life funds.

## WHOLE OF LIFE ASSURANCE

A whole of life policy is the most complicated of all the life assurances and can work out as the most expensive way to buy the life cover. There are two types of whole of life plans: *flexible whole of life* which qualify for tax relief on the payout when you die or surrender the policy, and *universal whole of life* plans which are non-qualifying. This means that you will have to pay income tax on the proceeds – but only at 40% – so if you normally pay 24% tax and the payout does not push you above the higher rate tax bracket, then there is no tax to pay.

Both universal and flexible whole of life plans allow you to choose the mix between life cover and investment you want. The three choices are maximum cover – with minimum investment; standard cover – where the investment and life cover are roughly equal; and minimum cover – with maximum investment. This can be changed throughout your life and you can increase the sum assured at certain points in your life such as when getting married, on the birth of a child or on moving house.

*Whole of life* plan providers allow you to add on a range of different options. If you choose one of these options and are struck down by the injury, illness or other incident covered by it then the policy will pay out before death (or pay extra). The main four are Permanent Total Disability Insurance, Critical Illness Cover, Permanent Health Insurance and Additional Accidental Death Benefit. These cover you against things such as being unable to work due to injury or sickness or contracting any one of a number of specified illnesses and conditions. The accidental death benefit will give an extra payout if your death was caused by an accident. See the CRITICAL ILLNESS INSURANCE GUIDE and PERMANENT HEALTH INSURANCE GUIDE for further details.

Life assurance is one of the most important financial products you can buy if you have anyone depending on you for an income. It is not expensive to buy pure life cover – either as term assurance or whole of life. Don't add to your family's grief by giving them money worries at the worst possible time.

Finally, you will still need life cover even if you do not have a family if you are going to borrow money. Otherwise your next of kin may be chased to repay the loan on your death.

# LONG-TERM CARE GUIDE

GROWING old and losing the ability to look after yourself is one of life's biggest fears.

Although no one likes to think about growing old it is one of life's certainties. But a little forward planning will make the transition to dependency on someone other than ourselves as stress free as possible.

While insurance can't help with the mental or physical trauma, it can help with the financial cost of growing old. As a pension provides an income in retirement, long-term care insurance will pay the cost of a nursing home or provide a home nurse if you do not want to move.

1. The cost of a stay in a residential nursing home is expensive – over £300 a week. And unless you start making provisions when you are young – in your forties or fifties – then long-term care insurance is also expensive.

There is no standard long-term care insurance policy. They differ both in the way they are funded – through a cash lump sum or regular monthly/annual payments – and in the products the money is invested in.

**2.** First, decide whether you want to remain at home, go into a nursing home or residential home when you become unable to look after yourself, or do you want to keep your options open?

Then decide how you want to fund your future care. Will it be out of income now, or through capital (maybe by the sale of your home) later? The funding method you choose will decide the plan that is best for you.

**3.** If you choose to fund out of income now, your money will be put into either an insurance fund, a unit or investment trust or an endowment policy. The first and last options are explained more fully in the LIFE ASSURANCE GUIDE, while the other two have their own guides.

When you need the care, the money will also be used to fund an annuity (see the ANNUITY GUIDE for further details). That said, all the plans currently on the market are different, and you should speak to a financial adviser (see the ADVISERS GUIDE) for precise details of each plan.

**4.** Before you take out a plan, also ask about your options. What happens if you change your mind and want to remain at home rather than stay in a nursing home? Or want to go home once you have moved into one? If you die before needing help, will there be a refund?

It is also worth checking who the money is paid to when the time comes. If it is direct to the nursing/residential home then it is tax free. But if it is paid to you and then on to the nursing home – or anyone who comes to your home to nurse you – then income tax is payable.

5.     One of the more standardised aspects of the long-term care plans currently available is the proof they require that you are unable to look after yourself.

The majority of companies require you to be unable to do, unassisted, two or three (depending on the company) activities of daily living (ADLs as they are known). These are: washing and bathing; using the toilet; dressing; continence; mobility and feeding.

The companies also test for senility via short- and long-term memory tests and orientation as to time and place. This ensures that people suffering from Alzheimer's disease or other forms of pre-senile dementia are not excluded from care.

Finally, the other alternative to taking out long-term care insurance is to use your home to provide the money to pay for care. This method is explained in the HOME INCOME PLAN GUIDE earlier in this section.

# MORTGAGE GUIDE

THE vast majority of people will end up owning – or joint owning – their own house at some point in their lives. Whether you are buying a one-bedroomed flat in London, a house in Norwich or a mansion is Buckinghamshire, the process of taking out a mortgage is exactly the same. The only difference is the amount of noughts added on to the end of the amount of money you are borrowing.

1. The first thing to do – before you even start looking at houses – is to work out how much you can afford to pay. Lenders, whether banks, building societies or centralised mortgage lenders, work on a formula based on earnings. The normal one is three times your earnings if you are buying alone – though some companies will go as high as three and a half times earnings. If you are buying with your spouse or partner, the equation normally becomes three times first earnings plus one times second, or even two and three-quarters times joint earnings.

Most mortgage lenders require a minimum of 5% of the value of the property as a deposit – though 100% mortgages are available. If you are self-employed, getting a mortgage is slightly more difficult, as you have to provide the would-be lender with three years' accounts (though some will accept less) as proof of income. If you are employed on a contract basis, as many people are these days, you have to be able to show that the contract will be renewed before a lender will offer money.

**2.** Once you have decided how much you can afford – and have cash saved up to pay for all the extra costs such as valuations and land registry fees – then it is time to look for your dream home. Remember that Stamp Duty must be paid at 1% on loans above £60,000.

The first £30,000 of a mortgage qualifies for mortgage interest relief – known as MIRAS – currently at 15%. You can also buy insurance to cover you against accident, sickness and unemployment, which will pay out until you are eligible for State relief.

The different ways of paying back a loan can be split into two: repayment and interest only. But there are many different ways of actually borrowing the money – fixed rate, variable, discounted, low-start and capped loans.

## REPAYMENT MORTGAGE

This is the simplest way to repay a mortgage loan. Each month your payments go towards paying back both the interest and the capital on the loan. It is estimated that the first 13-odd years of a 25-year mortgage are spent paying off the interest with the remainder paying off the capital. You can choose the length of time you want to take the loan out for.

No life insurance is attached to the loan, so you should take out cover – called term assurance – for the duration of the mortgage. This can either be level – covering the same amount of money over the term – or decreasing, which reduces each year in line with the amount of money you owe.

The next three mortgages are what is called interest only. This means the monthly payments you make are split into two. The bulk goes to cover the interest on the loan – you do not pay back any of the capital during the mortgages life – while the remainer is used to fund the repayment vehicle – the endowment, PEP or pension.

## INTEREST ONLY ENDOWMENT MORTGAGE

This has traditionally been the most popular form of repayment. Each month part of your payment is used to fund the premiums of an endowment policy. The different types of endowment policy are explained in full in the LIFE ASSURANCE GUIDE earlier in this section.

## INTEREST ONLY PERSONAL EQUITY PLAN (PEP) MORTGAGE

Like endowment mortgages, part of your monthly payment is used to pay off the interest charged on the loan, while the other part goes to fund the repayment vehicle.

A PEP mortgage is a way of investing in the Stockmarket tax free. The most usual method is through a unit trust or investment trust (see their different guides in this section) with a tax-free PEP wrapper, but you can choose the shares you want to invest in if you have the time and inclination. (See the PEP GUIDE for more details.)

PEPs do not have life cover included, so you will have to take out a life policy to cover the amount loaned.

## INTEREST ONLY PENSION MORTGAGE

Again the monthly payments are split into two – but in this case the second portion is invested into a pension. You will need to take out any extra life cover – regardless of whether your pension has this built in. The idea of a pension mortgage is that you continue to pay the interest on the loan until you retire. At this point part of the tax-free lump sum you receive is used to pay off the mortgage.

**3.** Once you have decided on the repayment vehicle for your mortgage then you have to decide on the type of loan – buying a house is not listed as one of the three most stressful times of your life for nothing!

The types of loan can be divided into five: variable, fixed, discounted, capped and low-start rates. What you choose will depend on the deals around at the time of taking out the loan and your individual circumstances.

## VARIABLE RATE

This is the most common type of mortgage loan. The amount you pay each month is based on the underlying base rate – set by the Government – and it will go up and down in line with this.

## FIXED RATE

On this type of loan the amount of interest you pay each month is fixed for a certain period of time – normally one to ten years – and normally the longer the rate is fixed, the higher the interest that will be charged. After the fixed term finishes you will either have the option to take out another fixed rate or revert to the lender's variable rate mortgage.

## DISCOUNTED RATE

This type of loan is linked to the lender's variable rate but you are given a discount off it. The discount is offered for a set period of time and, as with a fixed rate, the loan will revert back to the lender's full variable rate when it ends.

## CAPPED RATE

A capped rate mortgage is one where you agree with your lender a ceiling for the amount of interest you will pay. This ceiling is kept in place for an agreed amount of time and you will only ever have to pay up to the upper limit. If base rates fall during the agreed period, you pay the actual variable rate the lender is offering.

## LOW-START RATE

For first-time buyers especially, this is a way of deferring payments until your income has increased. The loan is normally linked to an endowment plan as the method of repayment. For the first, normally two, years, you do not pay the endowment premiums. These are funded by the lender and you build up a second loan made up of the cost of the premiums you are not paying.

After the low-start term has finished you start to pay the endowment policy as well as the interest on both the loans. Both loans will be paid off at the end of the life of the mortgage.

Before you sign on the dotted line for any of the special deals mentioned above, check the penalties if you want to get out of the mortgage. Many lenders set penalties of up to six months' interest payments if you want to pay off the loan, or move to another lender, either while the deal is ongoing, or for several years after.

There are also solicitors' costs for drawing up the mortgage agreement and the cost of a survey and valuation. You will also have to pay the cost of registering the deeds with the Land Registry and Stamp Duty at 1% of the purchase price if the value of the property is above £60,000, and it is all beginning to get expensive.

There is also the cost of the mortgage indemnity insurance – this is paid in one go on the portion of the loan above 75% of the loan to the value of the property, and covers the lender against your not paying the mortgage. If you are repossessed and the property is sold at a loss, then the insurer offering the mortgage indemnity policy can chase you for the shortfall.

4.    Once you have bought your house and are about to move in, the final thing to buy is home contents and buildings insurance. These are explained fully in the HOME INSURANCE GUIDE.

5.    Finally, your mortgage can be increased at any time if you want to make home improvements such as building an extension or renovating a loft. Alternatively, you can take out a personal loan, secured against the property (see the BANK GUIDE), or if you can repay quickly – within a year – you may be able to fund the improvements via your credit card.

Only the main types of mortgage are mentioned in this chapter. For a loan linked to a foreign currency, for example, you will need to see a mortgage adviser.

# NATIONAL SAVINGS GUIDE

NATIONAL Savings are the safest form of investment you can make. The only chance of not getting your money back is if the British Government goes bust!

National Savings offer ten different types of savings product – most of which are tax free. Here are the basics – for detailed information booklets are available from the Post Office.

## INDEX-LINKED SAVINGS CERTIFICATES

These offer a guaranteed rate of return for five years. During the five years your money increases both by the amount of inflation – measured by the Retail Price Index (RPI) – and a preset, fixed amount of bonus (interest). These increases are added each year and the next year's increase is based on the total amount (not just your original investment). If you wish to leave your money invested after year five, the interest rate will vary with other current rates, though the index linking will remain.

## FIXED INTEREST SAVINGS CERTIFICATES

With these certificates, the interest rate is fixed at the outset and the proceeds are paid tax free. The certificates are designed as a five-year investment but withdrawals can be made at any time. No interest is paid to new investors until the end of the first year – though people reinvesting other matured certificates will receive interest every three months.

## CHILDREN'S BONUS BOND

This five-year bond is available to all children up to the age of 16 and the returns are tax free. Withdrawals can be made and one month's notice is needed to take all the money out of the bond. If this is done in the first year no interest is payable.

## CAPITAL BONDS

The Capital Bond works in a similar way to the certificates mentioned above BUT it is taxable. Interest is paid to you gross but you must declare it to the Inland Revenue and pay tax on it each year – if you are a taxpayer. The bond is designed as a five-year investment but interest is paid annually and you get the money in year five.

## PENSIONER'S GUARANTEED INCOME BOND

This is a lump sum investment. It is designed to be held for five years and interest is paid gross monthly. This means you have to declare it to the Inland Revenue and pay tax on it at your highest rate. It is open to anyone aged 60 or over and money can only be got out with a 60-day notice period. If you want all your money back, no interest is paid during those 60 days.

## FIRST OPTION BONDS

This is a one-year investment with a fixed rate of interest. The FIRST stands for Fixed Interest Rate Savings Tax-paid which means that tax has already been paid before you get your money. If you are a non-taxpayer it can be reclaimed from the Inland Revenue.

Anyone over 16 can hold a bond and the money can be taken out at each anniversary without penalty. Encashing your money before the end of the first year means that no interest is paid. After this, withdrawals are entitled to half the quoted rate of interest from the period between the last anniversary and when the withdrawal is made.

## INCOME BONDS

These bonds pay a regular gross monthly income and are especially suitable for older people and people who pay no tax. The interest rate varies in line with base rates, so it will change – but National Savings must give you six weeks' notice of any changes.

## INVESTMENT ACCOUNT

This is the National Savings equivalent of a bank savings account. Anyone can set up an account and the interest is credited on 31 December each year. A bank book is issued with each account and this can be sent to National Savings Head Office in Glasgow to have the up-to-date balance written in. Alternatively, a yearly statement can be sent to you.

Money can be withdrawn via the Post Office or by post at any time but 30 days' interest is lost, or it takes one month from when the request is received by National Savings Head Office.

## ORDINARY ACCOUNT

An Ordinary Account is the National Savings equivalent of a bank current account – though you are given a bank book rather than a cheque book or cash card.

Money can be withdrawn every day via the Post Office or by post and you can also pay bills normally paid at the Post Office, such as TV licence or road tax, provided they are no more than £250, direct from your account. The interest is partially taxable, so taxpayers should declare it to the Inland Revenue.

## PREMIUM BONDS

These are a way of investing in a lottery but without losing your stake money. Anyone can invest in premium bonds whether for themselves or as an alternative to a cash gift. The bonds are entered into the draw after one calendar month and the numbers are picked each month by ERNIE (Electronic Random Number Indicator Equipment). Prizes range from £50 to £1 million a month and winners are notified by post.

National Savings also provide a service allowing you to buy or sell gilts (Government stocks which pay a fixed return) by post. See the SHARE GUIDE for further details on gilts.

# PEP GUIDE

ONCE you have sorted out all the insurance you need and have money saved in a bank or building society for short-term savings and emergency money, it is time to start looking at long-term investments.

Personal equity plans (PEPs) offer a tax-free way of saving up to £9,000 each year. All the income you take from them is tax free and when you come to sell your PEP and take the money, all the money you make (called capital gains) is free of tax as well. The PEP year runs from 6 April to 5 April alongside the tax year, not the calendar year.

PEPs are not an investment in themselves. They are a tax-free wrapping that you can put around investments in a unit trust, investment trust or direct shareholdings or bonds. This means that to understand this guide you need to read it in conjunction with the UNIT TRUST GUIDE, INVESTMENT TRUST GUIDE and SHARE GUIDE.

Anyone over 18 can invest in a PEP and there are rules governing the types of investment you can put into one. Your PEP investment is split into two. Up to £6,000 can be invested in a PEP investing in a qualifying unit trust, investment trust or directly into shares or corporate bonds. A further £3,000 can be invested into a single company PEP whereby you hold up to £3,000 in only one company – such as Marks & Spencer's shares.

To qualify for a full £6,000 PEP investment, a unit trust or investment trust must invest at least 50% of its money in the shares of UK or European companies or qualifying corporate bonds. The remainder can be invested anywhere in the world.

If you choose to invest your money directly into shares – known as a self-select PEP – then there is no limit to the number of different shares you can hold on the UK Stockmarket. Investment in European stockmarkets is also allowed, but can be quite tricky and expensive, so most people avoid it.

1. Do you want to invest for income, capital growth or a mixture of the two?

2. What you want from your investment will guide the choice of PEP you take out. You should also have a think about where you want your money invested – in the UK, Europe or as internationally spread as the rules will allow. You can invest in a non-qualifying unit or investment trust (ie. one with less than 50% in the UK or Europe), but this reduces the amount of money you can invest in a trust through a PEP to £1,500 from £6,000.

3. There are two ways to invest in a PEP, either as a lump sum of up to £6,000 or on a monthly basis – the maximum being £500 a month to keep inside the limit. You may be able to mix and match, paying in lump sums as and when you can afford to in addition to the monthly payments, but not every company offers these facilities, so check before you sign up.

**4.** Check the charges levied by the fund manager or stockbroker running your PEP, but don't buy a PEP on price alone. It is better to pay a little more if need be for a good performing fund than buy the cheapest if it is not going to produce any money for you.

**5.** In addition to the general £6,000 PEP mentioned above, you can also take out a single company PEP each year – investing up to £3,000. This is done by your choosing the company you want to invest in – such as British Telecom – and getting a stockbroker or PEP manager to invest in it for you. Existing shareholdings can also be put into a PEP (though the PEP manager will have to sell them and then buy them back to do so). The exception is if you want to invest in the company you work (or worked) for and get the shares through your employer's share option or profit-sharing scheme. The golden rule to remember is that the shares of only one company can be held in a single company PEP, though you can change the company as often as you like.

**6.** Falling in between the two PEP plans mentioned above is the corporate PEP. This works under the general PEP rules in that you can invest up to £6,000 a year, but you can only hold the shares of one company. Corporate PEPs are run on behalf of the company itself, rather than for you, and are normally open to employees of the company or existing shareholders. For example, British Airways runs a corporate PEP to allow people to invest in its shares, and once in a corporate PEP you cannot change the shares to a different company, as with a single company PEP. Single company and corporate PEPs are likely to have lower charges than general PEPs, as the costs of administering a portfolio with only one share in it are cheaper than one with lots of different shares.

# PERMANENT HEALTH INSURANCE GUIDE

IF you were unable to work because of a long-term sickness or disability, could you afford to pay the mortgage and the bills?

If the answer to this question is no, then you should look at taking out Permanent Health Insurance (PHI). This insurance is designed to pay a monthly income – like a wage – when you cannot work.

But it is not appropriate for everyone. If you earn less than £15,000 and especially if you are married with children then you will not be financially worse off living on State benefits.

1. The first thing to do is to decide a) whether you need this type of insurance, and b) how much of it you can afford.

Most companies will allow you to insure for the replacement of normally 75% of the first £30,000–£50,000 of gross earnings (the limit is usually £45,000) and 33.3% of the rest. Deducted from this is the single person's invalidity benefit and sometimes all other sources of income from other insurances/pension or earnings.

As a tip, most experts say insuring 30%–50% of your gross earnings is enough when all the other benefits are taken into account. This is one type of insurance that it does no good to over-insure yourself with. This is because you will only ever be paid out 75% of your gross income LESS any other forms of income regardless of the amount you have actually insured yourself for.

**2.** Decide how long you want to wait before the benefits become payable. This deferred period, as it is known, can range from four weeks to two years. In between the options are 8 weeks, 13 weeks, 26 weeks and one year.

**3.** The next thing to do is to decide what type of policy you want. The policy types can be split into five: guaranteed, reviewable, renewable, unit-linked and with-profits.

**4.** The final thing to choose is what level of disability you will have to be suffering before you are paid.

This splits into three groups: the first, and the one that costs the most, is 'unable to perform your own occupation'. The second, which is slightly cheaper, is 'unable to perform your own occupation or one suitable by education, training and experience'.

The third, and cheapest, of the options is 'unable to perform any occupation whatsoever'. This definition unfortunately means that you would have to be severely disabled or ill to qualify for a payout.

**5.** There are all sorts of other options that can be added. Cover can, and should, rise in line with inflation as measured by the retail price index (RPI) each year. Also check whether you can increase your insurance on events such as getting married or having children.

Also check the exclusions which are numerous on this type of policy. Some companies will cancel the policy on diagnosis of AIDS or HIV regardless of whether a claim is made, while others will cancel the policy if you spend long periods of time out of the country.

The other major set of exclusions relate to the job you do. The more dangerous it is, the harder it will be to get cover.

**6.** Once you start claiming, no tax is payable on the benefit (but only on personal policies not company ones); at this point your waiver of premium cover also kicks in and you will no longer have to pay the premiums while you are claiming.

**7.** Once you have taken out the plan, most companies require you to let them know if you change jobs. Not doing so could invalidate your cover.

**8.** When you come to claim, the payments will be made after your chosen deferred period and will continue until retirement (either 60 or 65 years old depending on the company).

# PERSONAL
# ACCIDENT GUIDE

AS anyone who has ever broken a leg will know, it is not just the pain that is a problem – it is the sheer inconvenience of it. The simple act of going up and down stairs becomes a major exercise, not to mention trying to put a pair of trousers on.

To help, the life insurance industry has come up with a policy designed to pay out specifically if you are involved in an accident – from hurting your thumb skiing to being involved in a car accident. It is called personal accident insurance and is one of the least expensive insurances you can buy.

1. Most insurers offer personal accident insurance and it will pay out when you have an accident – with the cash amount scaled to the severity of the injury. It will also pay out a set amount on death – but should not be used as a substitute for life cover.

One of its most important uses is as a family insurance. If your daughter or son, or spouse or partner, was badly injured, the chances are you would want to stay home and look after them. Having a cash payout means that you can afford to do this. The cash lump sum, or a weekly/monthly income if you prefer, is yours to do with as you like and it is paid tax free.

**2.** Many personal accident plans will also pay out if you are hospitalised or confined to the home. This takes the form of a cash payout of, say, £30 for each day incapacitated. The plan may also have legal expenses cover to pay the cost of any court action resulting from the accident.

# PERSONAL PENSION GUIDE

THERE is no point working hard all your life to improve your standard of living if, on retirement, it sinks to its lowest point because you have not set aside any money to live on once you stop work. This is why a pension is one of the most important financial products you will ever buy.

Pensions are not complicated – though they sometimes appear so. They are simply a way for you to set aside money to provide an income when you retire. And to encourage you to do this, the Government lets you put the money in tax free and the money you build up in your pension also grows tax free. As a safeguard, once you have put the money into a pension it cannot be touched until you retire. Taking out a personal pension or company pension will not stop your getting a State pension – it is designed to supplement it, not replace it.

There are two ways of saving for retirement – either through a company scheme which is explained in the COMPANY PENSION GUIDE or through a personal pension which is explained in this chapter. There are two types of personal pension around: old-style ones available before 1 July 1988, known as Section 226 plans, Section 620 plans or retirement annuity contracts; or new-style personal pensions. Only new-style personal pensions are dealt with in this chapter, as they are the only ones currently available.

Briefly, the basic difference between company and personal pensions is that a company scheme is run by your employer and you may pay into it only while you work for the company, while a personal pension belongs to you and can be taken from job to job. You can only pay into one of the different types of pension at any one time – except in set circumstances:

The State pension is made up of two parts – the basic amount which all will receive, provided they have paid enough National Insurance contributions, and the SERPS element. Self- employed people do not qualify for SERPS, so cannot contract out of it. Get professional advice before you contract out of SERPS, as it is not a good idea for everybody.

SERPS is the 'extra part' of the State pension which is linked to the amount of years you have worked and is based on one-fifth of your lifetime earnings. If you contract out, the Government will give you the money that has accumulated over the years you have worked plus a little bit extra (about 1% if you are over 30) to put into your own pension plan. It will also continue to pay in the amount that would have been the SERPS element of your State pension each year. If you have a company scheme, when you contract out you cannot put extra money (above the SERPS payment) into the personal pension.

You can find out how much SERPS rights you have built up so far and what your payments would be if you stayed in it until you retire by filling in the application form in the leaflet *'Your Future Pension'* (leaflet NP38 available from your local Social Security office).

You can only pay into a pension if you are earning. The

earnings can be anything from a full-time job to answering the telephone for your partner's business and doing a bit of typing in your spare time. Don't worry if you don't earn enough to pay tax or National Insurance, you can still take out your own pension – and get tax relief on the contributions (the money you pay in).

1. If you are aged between 16 and 75 you can take out a personal pension through a financial services company. Which one you take depends on your individual circumstances and you should always see a financial adviser before making a decision (see the ADVISERS GUIDE for the different types of advice available).

   As a rule of thumb, a company scheme will normally be much better than a personal pension so check exactly what your employer offers before taking out a personal pension. That said, for someone who is self-employed or intends to change jobs frequently, then a personal pension may well be the better option.

2. A personal pension works on what is known as a 'money purchase' basis. This means that the amount of money in your pension pot when you retire depends on how much you have put in and how quickly it has grown (known as the investment return). It is not guaranteed to give you a fixed amount when you retire and use it to buy an annuity. See the ANNUITY GUIDE for further details.

3. Before you take out a personal pension think about what you need.

   - The most important question is: how do you want to pay into your pension: monthly, yearly or on an ad hoc basis? The way you pay will affect the charges and will play a large part in your decision as to which company you use to run your pension. The options are a regular premium plan – whereby you pay a fixed amount each month or year (or other times with some plans), or a single premium plan – whereby you can make one-off payments for as much as you like whenever you like. Also decide when you would like to retire – a personal pension can be taken any time between the age of 50 and 75.

The State retirement age for both men and women is being equalised at 65 from the year 2010. This means that all women born after 6 April 1955 will not get their State pension until they reach 65, while those born between 6 April 1950 and 6 April 1955 will have their retirement date put back from 60 by a preset period of time.

- Do you want life cover included in your pension? Up to 5% of your earnings can be used to buy life cover – a cash lump sum payout to whomever you want if you die before you retire – and the premiums are tax free.

- Do you need to write your pension plan in trust? This means that when you die the money paid out will be separate from the rest of your estate and will not be tied up while inheritance tax is being paid and the estate sorted out. The named beneficiary cannot be changed by the life company in this case.

- Do you want the pension to continue to be paid to your spouse or children when you die?

4. The Government will give you tax relief at your highest rate. This means that if you pay 24% tax, for every £76 you pay in – from your taxed income – the Inland Revenue will pay £24, making a £100 contribution. If you pay higher rate tax at 40%, you should tell your local tax office – fill out form PP120 – and the extra relief above the standard rate of 24% will be credited to you. If you are self-employed then you pay your contributions in full (ie. the full £100 in the

example above) and tell the tax office when you fill in your income tax return. You will then be given a refund of the money or your tax assessment (the amount you owe) will be reduced by this amount. Also, for pension purposes, the 20% tax band is ignored, so you will be given a minimum of 24% tax relief regardless of what rate you actually pay below this, if any.

5. Many pension providers set the minimum and maximum amounts you can pay into your pension each month or year. But there are further limits that relate to the amount you earn – this is defined as your wages before tax, although any contributions you pay in will be net (after) tax. The maximum cash amount you can put into a new-style pension in the 1996/7 tax year is £82,200 – but below this the amount is worked out as a percentage of your earnings against your age. The percentages range from 17.5% for people under age 35 to 40% for people aged 61–74.

Your employer can pay into your personal pension for you (but not into an old-style one) provided the maximum percentage is not exceeded. If you do pay in more than your allowed amount in any one year, it will be paid back to you as soon as possible. If you do choose to take out life cover within the pension, the amount it costs you each year is treated as a pension payment and is subject to the same maximums.

Although these are the usual limits, there are ways of paying in more than the maximum percentage of your earnings listed below in a single year. The system is known as 'carry back' and 'carry forward'.

*Carry forward* allows you to count up your unused tax relief for the previous six years and use it as an extra contribution in the current year. This means, for example, that if you are under 35 and have only paid in 10% of your income for the past six years, you would have the cash equivalent of 7.5% of your earnings left over each year to pay in as a tax-free lump sum. This system was designed for those people who start paying into a personal pension late into their careers, as it gives them the opportunity to catch up.

*Carry back* relief allows you to ask the Inland Revenue to treat the money you have paid into your pension this year as if you put it in last year. For example, if you only paid the equivalent of 7% of your income into a pension last year (and are under 35) but are able to afford to pay in more this year, you can ask for the extra – up to the 17.5% limit, ie. 10.5% of income – to be treated as if you paid it in last year. This means it will be given tax relief at the tax rate in force last year and will allow you to make extra contributions next year and carry them back if you want. But you must ask for this to be done within three months of the end of the tax year and it can only be done if you were self-employed that year or did not pay into your employer's pension scheme. You can normally only carry back contributions one year.

**6.** Once you get to your chosen retirement age you have two choices for your personal pension – either to take up to 25% as a tax-free cash lump sum and use the remainder to buy an annuity to provide you with an income until you die; or use the whole pension pot to buy an annuity. The money you receive from the annuity is taxed as income.

You can use the tax-free cash lump sum for anything you like – paying off the mortgage, buying a new car or going on holiday – but the remaining money must be used to buy an annuity. This can either be from the company that ran your pension or from any other annuity provider in the market. It is worth shopping around before you buy your pension annuity, as the rates do vary from company to company and once you have bought an annuity you cannot switch providers at a later date.

It is also possible to defer purchasing an annuity until you reach the age of 75. In this case, your pension fund remains invested after your retirement and you draw an income from it. The maximum amount you can take as income is calculated with reference to a Government standard and pensions opting for income drawdown can take between 35% and 100% of this sum per year. This facility is intended to allow pensioners to choose the most advantageous time to buy a retirement annuity.

# PRIVATE MEDICAL INSURANCE GUIDE

AS time goes on, the Welfare State is becoming less and less able to fulfil its promise of cradle to grave health care. In recognition of this, a plethora of private independent hospitals have been built offering medical treatment – but at a price.

To help you pay this price, the insurance industry has designed a policy called Private Medical Insurance. This basically pays for you to be treated in one of the private hospitals and will pay you cash if you have your operation on the NHS.

1.  There are two core types of plan – comprehensive and budget – but within these two divisions every plan is different, making financial advice imperative.

    As the name suggests, a comprehensive plan covers you for all hospital costs, outpatients' fees and fees levied by specialists. It will also pay for alternative medicines such as homeopathy and acupuncture, and for pregnancy and childbirth. Both these and the budget plans will also give you a cash sum (of around £50) for every night you spend in an NHS hospital.

A budget plan covers a lot less. Normally you are offered private treatment if the operation you need has a six weeks or more waiting list via the NHS, but gives full cover while you are in hospital. A subsection of the budget plan is the hospital care or inpatients' plan which only covers you while you are a patient in the hospital and any outpatient treatment related to this.

In between these two extremes are the standard plans. These cover the inpatient and surgeons' fees as with the budget plans, but also home nursing, outpatients' fees, private ambulance and cash refunds.

Finally, there are some plans on the market designed for the over sixties who are given tax relief by the Government as an incentive to make their own provisions. There are certain restrictions on these plans. For example, if you receive tax relief on the premiums you are not allowed to receive cash benefits for staying in an NHS hospital, cover for alternative medicine or cover for dental and eye treatment – unless this requires a stay in hospital. Anyone can take out a PMI plan on behalf of someone over 60 and get the tax relief – limited to 24% though – and for married couples only one partner needs to be over 60 to qualify.

**2.** The major drawback to most plans is that they will not cover existing medical conditions, pregnancy or dental treatments (such as having a filling or a crown fitted). Some companies will, however, allow what is known as a moratorium. This is when existing conditions will be covered after a certain number of years provided a claim (or often a related claim) has not been made during the preset period.

# RENT GUIDE

WHEN you first move out of your parents' home it is unlikely that it will be straight into a property you own. It is possible that you will become a tenant.

1. There are a few ground rules to follow before you even start looking. Decide:

   • How much rent you can afford to pay each week or month and stick by it.
   • Whether you want to live with people or on your own.
   • What type of property you want to rent.
   • What area you want to live in.
   • How close you want to be to the buses and trains.

2. You will have to pay at least one month's rent as a deposit against any damage when you leave, plus a month's rent in advance. If you found the property through an agent (either flat share or letting), you may also have to pay a fee to them.

3.  Your new landlord will probably ask for references – one from your bank and another from your last landlord or employer. At the same time you can ask for testimonies from previous tenants and for the deposit to be put into a separate bank account.

    You will also be asked to sign a contract. Read the contract very carefully. If you do not fully understand it then get someone who does to read it for you and explain what each part means.

    Before you sign the contract find out who is responsible for the maintenance of the property. If the roof starts to leak, the toilet overflows or you find yourself sharing the house with silverfish and cockroaches, whose problem is it? Get this written into the contract if isn't already, as it will save a lot of heartache should something go wrong at a later date.

4.  Make sure you get an inventory, listing everything in the flat, sign it and get it signed by the landlord. This will stop any arguments over what was and wasn't included when you move out.

5.  Take out home contents insurance to cover your own possessions. See the HOME INSURANCE GUIDE for further details of how the insurance works.

# SCHOOL FEES PLANNING GUIDE

ALL parents want their children to have a better start in life than they had – be it more toys or, more importantly, a better education. But sending your child to a private school can be an expensive exercise. School fees can cost well over £1,000 a term and are rising at a rate of nearly 10% a year – way above the actual rate of inflation.

But you don't have to be a multi-millionaire to send your child to a private or independent school. You will have to do a little forward planning though, if you don't want to see your standard of living fall in order to pay the fees each term.

There are five ways of paying for school fees:

- Future funding from capital
- Future funding from income
- Immediate funding from capital
- Immediate funding from income

- Out of borrowings or third-party finance
(such as grandparents or remortgaging your home)

Many of the best schools have such a long waiting list that you have to put his/her name down almost before your child is born. School fees planning should be treated in exactly the same way. The longer you plan and save, the less of your own money you will actually have to use.

But don't despair if you think you have left it too late and it is only a few months or years before your child is due to start at a private school; there are ways of getting round the problem.

There are a whole range of different products that can be used to pay off school fees. Some are specifically designed for the task while others, such as with-profits endowments, can be adapted. Exactly which products are used depends on your personal circumstances and you should get professional advice before doing anything. The ADVISERS GUIDE explains the different types of advice available.

If you can afford it, it is also worth taking out some sort of protection insurance while you are paying school fees – just in case either you or your partner or spouse are unable to work through sickness, injury, unemployment or death. Many schools offer their own redundancy plans which may be cheaper than those on offer from insurance companies, so ask around before you buy. If you want to find out more about these protection insurances have a look at the PERMANENT HEALTH INSURANCE GUIDE, CRITICAL ILLNESS GUIDE and LIFE ASSURANCE GUIDE.

Listed on page 187 are some of the main options used to pay off school fees, though it is not a definitive list. The first two mentioned are specifically designed to pay off school fees.

## EDUCATIONAL TRUSTS

These trusts are designed for parents with capital that they can invest as a lump sum some years before their child is due to start school. The trusts are run by insurance (life) companies in the main and the money is invested in a managed fund or safe type of investment until it is needed.

A managed fund is an insurance fund run by the life company which invests in a whole range of shares, other investment funds and investments that pay a fixed amount of income. Your investment is pooled with other people's to spread the risk.

Once the money is needed to pay the school fees it is used to buy an annuity – this is a guaranteed income for a fixed period of time.

## COMPOSITION FEE SCHEMES

This is also a way of paying a cash lump sum in advance – but this time to the school that you have decided to send your child to. In return for giving it the money, the school will agree to freeze the fees at their current level or offer you reduced fees.

The money is used by the school to invest in an annuity and as with the educational trusts it can use its charitable status to invest tax efficiently.

On the insurance side a whole host of investment and insurance products are used, ranging from unit and investment trusts to with-profits endowments. The decision as to which to use is based on three factors: the time until the fees need to be paid; the amount of capital or income available to be invested; and the risk profile of the parents. (See the UNIT TRUST, INVESTMENT TRUST and LIFE ASSURANCE GUIDES for further details.)

## WITH-PROFITS AND UNITISED WITH-PROFITS ENDOWMENT

A with-profits, or unitised with-profits, endowment can either be bought using a lump sum of capital or by saving on a regular basis. It is a way of investing your money in a pool with other people's to invest in shares and other types of investment. Each year a bonus is paid (the reversionary bonus), which once given cannot be taken away. It is based on the investment return throughout the year. At the end of the life of the endowment a final bonus is paid (the terminal bonus) which boosts the return. An endowment can be taken out for whatever period of time you want. The basic difference for the investor between a unitised with-profits fund and a traditional with-profits fund is that the unitised one is divided into units, with the bonus being allocated to the number you own within the fund. With the traditional fund the money is put into one big pool and the bonus you receive depends on what percentage of the pot you own.

## UNIT TRUSTS, INVESTMENT TRUSTS AND PEPS

These are only suitable for people with a fairly long time to invest their money. Both unit trusts and investment trusts provide a way of pooling your money with other people's to invest in a wide range of shares and other types of investment. Investing this way helps to reduce the risk.

## BANK AND BUILDING SOCIETY ACCOUNTS, NATIONAL SAVINGS

Normal building society accounts are a good place to put your money if you don't like taking risks. The more money you have, and the longer you are willing to tie it up for, the higher the interest you will get. If you put the money into a TESSA – a Tax Exempt Special Savings Account which allows you to invest up to £9,000 over five years – the interest will also be paid tax free. See the BANK GUIDE,

BUILDING SOCIETY GUIDE and NATIONAL SAVINGS GUIDE for further details.

## REMORTGAGING YOUR HOME

Remortgaging your home is another option if school fees need to be paid instantly. If you are going to do this, make sure that you can afford the increased repayment each month or you could find yourself in arrears and having your home repossessed.

However, there are schemes that allow you to borrow in tranches against your home – like a home income plan (see the HOME INCOME PLAN GUIDE). This means that you only borrow what you need as you need it – reducing the amount of interest that you pay on the loan.

Alternatively, some companies will also allow you to take a loan out against an endowment policy – either one taken out specifically for this purpose or an existing one being used to pay off a mortgage.

# SHARE GUIDE

THE Stockmarket can be both fascinating and forbidding at the same time. But a little careful study and a working knowledge of how the Stockmarket works can get rid of the scariness and allow you to have fun.

1. Shares are simply a means of buying a part of a company – such as Marks & Spencer. When M&S was originally founded it was privately owned and you could not have bought shares in it. But as it grew and needed money to finance more growth, it floated itself on the Stock Exchange, offering people like you and me a chance to own a small part of it.

The reason people buy shares, either when the company initially floats or 'second hand' (known as the secondary market), is because they believe that the shares offer value for money, and that the company will continue to grow and increase its profits – paid out to shareholders in the form of dividends.

**2.** Although most of your other investments will have all or a high percentage invested in shares, you should not think about buying shares directly until you are adequately covered in other areas. Make sure that you have enough life cover, a pension and some money saved in the bank for emergencies before you put your money directly into shares.

**3.** There are some 20,000 different shares listed on the UK Stock Exchange alone, ranging from international conglomerates worth billions of pounds to small, UK-based companies worth only a few million. The prices of all these shares are listed each day in most of the newspapers and on TV-based services such as Ceefax and Teletext. The shares are divided into different sectors, such as industrial, chemical, food or property. It is because of this vast array of choice that it is important to do your homework before investing.

**4.** The most important rule is to spread the risk. The higher the risk, the higher the reward, but you have to decide what level of risk you are comfortable with.

**5.** Once you have decided that you want to invest in the Stockmarket then it is time to find yourself a stockbroker. There are three types of service available: execution only, advisory and discretionary.

The cheapest way to deal is through an execution-only stockbroker. With an execution-only stockbroker, you say what shares you want to buy and sell, and he or she will go away and do it for you. No advice is given and you can place your order via the telephone, by post or through local branches.

Many of the execution-only stockbrokers, as well as many others, will also offer an advisory service. This gives you someone to talk to about your decisions, ask advice of and often get access to the company's own research on the shares you are interested in. Ultimately, though, the final decision on what to invest in is yours.

Advisory services range from just having someone on the end of a telephone to face-to-face talks with your personal stockbroker, who will keep tabs on your portfolio and give regular valuations.

The final, and most expensive, type of stockbroking service is discretionary portfolio management. With this, you hand the responsibility for buying and selling shares, and managing your portfolio, over to a stockbroker.

**6.** If you hold shares directly then the dividend income is paid after 20% investment tax has been deducted. If you pay the higher rate of 40% then you must pay extra at the end of each tax year.

When you come to sell your shares you may also have to pay capital gains tax on any profits. This is payable on profits above £6,300 (for the 1996/7 tax year) at your highest rate of tax.

**7.** The most tax-efficient way of investing in shares is through a personal equity plan (PEP). This allows you to invest up to £9,000 a year in any qualifying shares you like, free of income tax or capital gains tax when you come to sell them. See the PEP GUIDE for further details of how PEPs work.

**8.** But shares are not the only things traded on the Stockmarket. You can also buy fixed interest securities (or bonds as they are often known). The most common are Government bonds (known as gilts), and they are issued by the Government to raise money to finance its spending programme. Although the price goes up and down once you have bought a gilt, the return you receive – normally twice yearly – is fixed at the outset. If you hold the bond until it matures, you will also receive £100 per gilt back.

**Bonds are issued by the larger companies as a way of raising money. These work in exactly the same way as Government gilts (though the amount you receive when the bond matures may not be £100), but are seen as more risky, as there may be a higher chance that the company will default and be unable to pay back the loan.**

If you like the idea of investing in the Stockmarket but do not feel confident enough to do it yourself – or do not have enough money to spread your risk – then it may be worth investing via a unit trust or investment trust. These offer a way of pooling your money with other investors and investing in a wider spread of shares than you could afford by yourself. See the UNIT TRUST GUIDE and INVESTMENT TRUST GUIDE for further details.

Alternatively, you could get together with a group of up to 20 friends and set up your own investment club. This is like a do-it-yourself unit trust. Each member invests an equal or pre-agreed amount and the money is invested in the Stockmarket. An organisation called ProShare runs the trade association for investment clubs and has books and leaflets to help (Tel: 0800 556622).

# TAX GUIDE

It is impossible to go through life without paying taxes for one thing or another.

For the workers, income tax and National Insurance take a healthy slice out of our wage packets each month. Other taxes such as value added tax (VAT) increase the Chancellor's kitty, not to mention tax on cigarettes, alcohol and petrol, to name but a few.

This guide lists some of the taxes that we pay. It is not definitive – for that you need to see an accountant or talk to the Inland Revenue.

The rates given are for the tax year 1996/97 which started on 6 April 1996.

*Income taxes and allowances:*

| | |
|---|---|
| Lower rate tax – 20% of taxable income | £1 – £3,900 |
| Basic rate – 24% | £3,901 – £21,600 |
| Higher rate – 40% | over £25,500 |
| Personal allowance – under 65 | £3,765 |
| Married couple's allowance – under 65 | £1,790* |
| Single parent allowance | £1,790* |

Widow's bereavement allowance          £1,790*

Blind person's allowance          £1,250*

*Relief restricted to 15% down from 20% in 1994/95*

Mortgage interest tax relief is 15% in respect of interest paid on the first £30,000 of a qualifying loan.

Capital gains tax (CGT): the annual exemption is £6,300. Gains in excess of this amount are taxed at the individuals highest tax rate.

# TRAVEL GUIDE

MOST people will go on holiday at least once in their lives, be it to Brighton or Barbados – and when you travel things can and do go wrong. Disasters range from flights being cancelled, to luggage being lost or your handbag stolen.

This is why it is important, but not compulsory, to take out travel insurance before you go. This covers you against a whole range of misadventures. The main areas are personal liability cover – if you damage someone or something; medical expenses while abroad; cancellation/curtailment of your holiday; loss of luggage and loss of passport and money.

1. There are two types of travel insurance – trip by trip cover and annual policies. Which one is best value for you depends on how often you travel each year. As with all types of insurance, what is covered and its cost vary from company to company, so it is worth shopping around before you go.

**2.** Before you sign up:

- Is there any holiday cover attached to your household insurance? If you have an all-risks policy it should cover your luggage and spending money while you are away. This will cut the cost of your travel insurance, but if you have to make a claim you may find the cost of your household insurance rises when you renew next year.

- Some credit cards come with free or low-cost travel insurance. Find out if yours does, how much it costs and what it covers.

- If you are going on an activities holiday make sure that the activities you intend to pursue are covered by your travel insurer.

- Make sure that the cash refund you get if the holiday is cancelled/ curtailed is enough to cover the actual cost of the holiday.

- What level of medical cover do you get with the policy? Is it appropriate to your destination?

- What level of personal liability cover do you have? Is it enough?

- Be truthful about any pre-existing medical conditions. If not, you could invalidate the cover if you have to make a claim.

- Is there a time limit on how long you have to make a claim?

**3.** Should disaster occur, get official confirmation on the spot. If belongings are stolen, a police statement will be needed as proof; for a medical claim, a medical certificate will be required; and if there is a problem with your flight or lost luggage, get a report from the airline carrier.

**4.** As extra protection – though it should not be used as a substitute for travel insurance – you can get an E111 form from your local Post Office. This entitles you to some free, on-the-spot medical cover when you travel in Continental Europe.

# TRUST GUIDE

TRUSTS have two main uses. They allow you to leave something – money, property, jewellery and any other possessions – to a person, without him or her having to pay inheritance tax (IHT) on your death. They also allow you to control what happens to these possessions by setting any conditions or minimum ages you want in order for the person to receive the gift.

You can also put money or other possessions into a trust, and have them paid out to someone else while you are alive – but there will be tax implications.

Trusts do not just have to be used to leave things to your family and friends. They can also be used in business, allowing you to put shares in the company or the part of it you own in a trust and thus outside your estate. This means that the people left behind to run your business – your partners or children – can get on with it without having to wait for the estate to be sorted out.

**1.** You should think about putting things into trust when you write your will (see the WILL GUIDE for advice on this). You can set up a trust in your will which comes into effect once you die. For example, you may want to leave your house to your children but allow your spouse or partner to live in it until he or she dies. In this case the house could be put into trust for your children. This would stop their being able to sell it before your partner dies, as it would be a condition of the will, and would also stop your partner's selling the house and spending the proceeds, thus depriving your children of their inheritance.

**2.** As you get older you should also think about the ways of reducing the inheritance tax (IHT), payable on the portion of an estate over the current IHT floor of £200,000, that your beneficiaries will have to pay once you die. It is here that trusts come into their own.

Once you have decided how much over the IHT threshold your estate will be, then you should take out a policy written in trust to cover this amount. Make sure that the life policy you use is flexible enough to allow you to increase the payout – known as the sum assured – over the years. The LIFE ASSURANCE GUIDE and the INHERITANCE TAX PLANNING GUIDE explain this idea in further detail.

**3.** A trust is just a wrapping put round a life policy or other item such as a house. Trusts fall into two camps: those that allow you to retain an interest such as receiving an income from them while you are still alive, and those that once put into trust are closed to you. Some will also allow you to change your mind on who benefits from them; others will not.

**4.**   Trusts have to be worded in a very specific way and before setting one up you should get professional financial (and often legal) advice. Most insurance companies provide standard trusts that can be used to wrap round a life policy and the ADVISERS GUIDE explains the different sorts of financial advice available.

Remember, a trust is not a trust if you take out the life policy for your own benefit, ie. you are the named beneficiary. In this case the money will be paid straight into your estate on death and will be liable to inheritance tax.

A policy written on a joint life, first death basis cannot be put into a trust. Again the money will form part of your estate on death. A policy that is assigned to a third party as security, such as an endowment policy that will be used to pay off your mortgage loan, cannot be put in trust. In the event of your death the money from the policy will be given to the loan company to do this.

**5.**   When you set up a trust, you have to name several sets of people within the trust document. The first is the beneficiary or beneficiaries. The second are the trustees, of which you can be one, and the third – which not all trusts allow – is a list of potential beneficiaries if, in time, you want to change your mind.

Below is a list of some of the main types of trust. It is not definitive and we cannot stress how important it is to get professional advice before taking any action.

- *Absolute Trust.* This gives the beneficiaries the absolute right to the money or other goods within the trust. It is not possible to change who benefits from the trust after setting it up.

- *Discretionary Trust.* This allows you to take an income from the money held inside it. You can also leave the money on your death to a wide number of potential beneficiaries.

- *Flexible Trust*. This allows you to adjust the amount of money within the trust that you want to give to the current and potential beneficiaries (the third group mentioned above).

- *Interest in Possession Trust*. With this, the beneficiaries have a right to the income paid on the investment in the trust as and when it is given. This right is known as an 'interest in possession'.

- *Pension Trust*. When you take out your pension you can also take out life cover – and get tax relief on the premiums. Since the pension itself is written under trust (and the life cover comes under the same rules in this case), you can make an expression of wish naming the person you would like to receive the money should you die before retirement.

- *Split Trust*. With this trust you can name two different sets of beneficiary who will get the money in different circumstances.

- *Will Trust*. This is a trust established under the terms of a will.

# UNIT TRUST GUIDE

MANAGING your money is as much about successfully prioritising how you spend it as not spending more than you actually have – and this is one of the most important points to remember with your savings.

The most important thing is to make sure that you have enough money tucked away in the building society to see you through an emergency and as rainy day money to pay for holidays and treats.

Once this is done, and you have adequate life cover and other forms of insurance, then it is time to look at a pension. See the other guides in this section for further details on all these types of savings and insurance.

Only when you have enough of these types of cover should you start to look at saving your money for the longer term. One of the best ways of doing this – and the one which will bring you a much higher return than anything the building society can produce, even when interest rates are high – is investing in the Stockmarket.

You can do this either by investing directly into shares (see the SHARE GUIDE earlier in this section) or through what is known as a collective investment. These take two main forms: a unit trust or an investment trust.

Both allow you to pool your money with that of other people's and invest in a wide spread of shares with no capital gains tax liability within the funds. This means that the risk is reduced because your £100 buys a part share in, say, 40 companies' shares, rather than fully owning just one or two. The differences between unit trusts and investment trusts are in the structure, not in the return you receive.

Remember, though, both these types of savings are for the long term. If you think you will need the money within five years then look at one of the shorter term investments. Have a look at the BOND GUIDE or the NATIONAL SAVINGS GUIDE for ideas.

Unit trusts can be used for a whole host of things – paying off your mortgage, paying school fees or just to save for some luxury like a faraway holiday.

1. The first thing to do is to decide if a unit trust is actually what you want and need. Ask yourself a series of questions before you start paying into one. Most importantly, can you afford to tie the money up for a long period of time? If so, will you need it after this to pay off a fixed amount – such as a mortgage loan? The value of your unit trust will go up and down, so if you need the money on a certain date you will have to think it through carefully.

2. There are two ways of saving into a unit trust: either via a lump sum of, say, £500 or £1,000 or through regular monthly amounts of as little as £20 through the trust's savings scheme. The savings scheme is a very flexible way of saving, as you can stop it without penalty at any time (and then restart it again when you can afford to), and you can still pay in lump sum amounts as and when you can.

3. Unit trusts can be divided into three main groupings: ones that provide an income; ones that invest for capital growth (the growth in the value of the money you invest – called the capital); and ones that provide a mixture of both. Income unit trusts will also provide a small level of capital growth and capital growth trusts may well produce a small amount of income, but if you need both then go for a balanced trust that chooses shares for both their income and capital growth potential.

Unit trusts are actually trusts which buy shares (and other types of investment) and package them into units. Each unit owns an equal part of the total amount of the shares – known as the portfolio. Any money you put in is used to buy these units and the value of them goes up and down in line with the value of underlying investments.

Investment trusts, on the other hand, are actually companies that are specifically designed to buy shares in other companies. The way the price of the investment trust shares is shown is slightly different to that of a unit trust as well, and for more information on investment trusts you should read the INVESTMENT TRUST GUIDE earlier in this section.

4. Unit trusts have been around for 60-odd years and come in every colour, shape and size. You can invest in anything from cash to coffee to gilts and bonds through them, and the amount of risk you take with your money is entirely up to you.

If you don't feel comfortable making your own choice of trust then you should get professional advice. The ADVISERS GUIDE explains the different types of advice available. If you do want to go it alone, then the Association of Unit Trusts and Investment Funds (AUTIF), Tel: 0181 207 1361, produces several useful guides including a list of the names and addresses of unit trust companies.

Alongside choosing whether you want income, capital or a

mixture of both from your investment, you should also decide how much risk you are willing to take with your money. If you will lose sleep if the value of your money falls by the smallest amount, then a unit trust investing in Mexico, for example, is probably not for you.

The prices and performance of all unit trusts are listed both in the newspapers, alongside the share prices, or in specialist financial magazines. The trusts are normally divided up into sectors – such as UK income or international balanced – so that you can compare the performance of different trusts with the others that are designed to do the same thing (eg. provide income from a similar set of investments).

When you are choosing a unit trust you should look at the return it has produced over the longer term (three to five years). Looking at the short term – six months or a year – is not a good indication of how well a trust will perform. If it is a launch of a new unit trust then you should look at how well similar trusts run by the same manager have performed to get an idea. Your final choice, however, should be based on both the performance of the trust and the charges levied by the managers for running it.

**5.** Once you have decided the fund you want to buy then it is time to contact the company that runs it and send it your money. Unit trusts carry an initial charge – known as the bid offer spread. This is the difference in the price that you can buy and sell the units at. It ranges from about 2% to 6% depending on the trust – though some companies offer discounts on the initial price to attract investors. Never buy a trust on price alone – if it is not a good performer then you will not make money regardless of how cheap it was.

Unit trusts also have annual management charges ranging from 0.75% to 1.5% or above. This is the most important charge, as it grows in line with your money. This means that the £100 you invest in a fund with an annual charge of 1% pays £1, but when it grows to £1,000 the charge will grow to £10 and so on.

You can also opt to invest in the trust via a personal equity plan (PEP). This allows you to receive all the income and capital growth tax free (see the PEP GUIDE for further details). If you do not use the PEP route then the income you receive from the trust will automatically be taxed. If you don't pay tax, it can be reclaimed, and if you should pay 40% tax on it then the extra will have to be paid at the end of the tax year. If you make a profit on the investment when you sell it of more than £6,300 (in the 1996/7 tax year) you will have to pay capital gains tax at either 24% or 40%, depending on what income tax you normally pay.

You can sell your investment whenever you want to for the market value of the units. Very few unit trusts guarantee that you will get your money back – if one does, it will say so before you buy it – so there is always a risk that you may not get all your money back if you cash in too early or when the markets are down. This is why you should hold the unit trust investment for as long as possible. But, historically, unit trusts have outperformed bank and building society accounts and should make your money work as hard for you as you did to earn it.

# WILL GUIDE

EVERYONE needs a will. You may not think that you have anything of value to leave – but what about the TV and stereo? If you don't leave a will they may be given to people whom you would not have chosen.

If you are not married but live with a partner it is doubly important, as there is no such thing as a 'common law spouse' under English law (though there is in Scotland).

1. The first thing to do is to sit down and decide who gets what on your death. Make a rough calculation of the value of your property – you don't have to be too precise because the value will change over the years. Don't forget to include the value of any life policies that pay out on death and deduct the amount of your mortgage if there is no life policy attached that will pay off the loan on your death.

If you die without a will then you die 'intestate'. There are very strict laws governing the property, known as an estate, of people who die without a will and you could, in extreme cases, find that you have left your whole estate to the Crown instead of to loved ones. This happens when there is no immediate family alive to give the estate to.

**2.** Next, decide who will be the executors of your will – to make sure your wishes are carried out. You may also need to appoint a guardian if you have young children. You can appoint anyone to be an executor of your will – most spouses appoint each other as they are best placed to know the details of the estate. If you do not want your spouse to be the executor of your will then you can choose a family friend, a solicitor or accountant, or even your bank. Make sure that you ask the person before appointing them as an executor as it is a very responsible job. On death an executor must work out the value of your estate minus its liabilities (any debts) and then administer it.

If you do not appoint an executor, your next of kin will normally be appointed to administer the estate (and be known as the administrator). The difference between these two is that an executor has the power to deal with an estate from the moment of death, whereas an administrator must wait until the courts grant Letters of Administration.

**3.** Once you have decided who will receive what, then it is time to actually draw up the will. This can be done with or without a solicitor – though it is always advisable to get help in these matters. You can get ready drawn-up wills with blank spaces for you to fill in your individual requirements from stationery shops. If you are choosing this route, make sure that there is enough space for you to set out your desires and that you understand what the will says.

Since a will is a technical legal document it is vital to get it right if you are doing it yourself. An incorrectly drawn-up will can lead to a long, expensive court case, should it be contested, which could vastly reduce the value of your estate when it is finally resolved.

While you are drawing up your will, it is important to bear in mind the inheritance tax implications of what you are doing. The current inheritance tax (IHT) floor is £200,000. Estates worth less than this are IHT free, while estates worth more will pay tax at 40% on the excess. That said, leaving all your possessions to your spouse is tax free, as are gifts to charities and gifts made more than seven years ago. The INHERITANCE TAX GUIDE explains the rules more fully and ways of reducing the potential tax bill.

Remember that there are two ways that your will can be contested. The first is if you disinherit someone who is financially dependent on you, ie. a child, or if you die intestate and a partner is left out because of the laws governing intestacy. The application to change the will must be made within six months of the granting of probate or Letters of Administration. The other way is through a Deed of Variation. This can be done within two years of your death and all the beneficiaries of your will must be in agreement. This is normally, though not always, done to reduce any tax implications.

**4.** Once written, the will must be witnessed by two people, and each page should be signed and dated in your presence. They cannot be people who are mentioned as beneficiaries in your will – if they are then they are automatically disinherited (this is not the case in Scotland). By the same token, witnesses to the will should not be the people who will execute it. This again disinherits them and stops their claiming any expenses they may run up in the execution of the will, though using someone from these two groups of people will not invalidate the will.

**5.** It is vital that you keep your will in a safe place. If you used a solicitor to help you draw up the will then he or she will also be able to store it for you. If not, put it somewhere safe – preferably with any other important documents, such as details of any life policies and the deeds of your house. A family safe at home, if you have one, is ideal or your bank and building society will store it for a small annual charge.

Do tell the executors of your will where all your papers are kept or there could be a mad search to find your will when you die, and if it can't be found, the laws of intestacy may apply, laying waste to your carefully laid plans.

If you don't have a safe place to put your will, it can be registered at the Probate Office. Write to the Record Keeper, Principal Registry, Family Division, Somerset House, Strand, London WC2R 1LP.

**6.** Your will can be changed at any time during your life. Additions to the will or a complete change can be done by adding a codicil, or if the changes are more complex, writing a new will altogether.

If your circumstances do change and a new will is drawn up, don't forget to add a clause revoking (scrapping) all previous wills. It is probably best to destroy the old will as well, or it may be mistaken for the one you want used. You must be present when an old will is destroyed or the revocation is not valid.

**7.** Remember to keep your will up to date at all times.

# SECTION 3:
# Wealth Check

# BUDGET PLANNER

THE chapters and guides in the first two sections of this book have explained the sorts of insurance and financial product available to you, when you need them and how they work. But if you don't have the money to buy them, it doesn't matter how good or appropriate they are for you.

To help you work out how much money you actually have, against how much you spend, this chapter gives a budget planner. Listed in the following pages are all the outgoings you may have each month (or use it for the year if you prefer) and all the different sources of income. Taking the outgoings from the income will show you if you have anything left over or any areas of overspending.

We have also compiled an asset planner which lets you list all your assets such as pensions, life policies and your home. This will let you keep a rough tally of what you are worth, for inheritance tax purposes or just as a record.

## BUDGET PLANNER
*INCOME*

| | |
|---|---|
| Salary | £ ........................................ |
| Bonus and other benefits | £. ........................................ |
| Income from investments | £ ........................................ |
| Interest from savings | £ ........................................ |
| Other (eg. maintenance) | £ ........................................ |
| **Total Income** | £ ........................................ |

*OUTGOINGS*
*Housing costs:*

| | |
|---|---|
| Mortgage/rent | £ ........................................ |
| Service charge/ground rent | £ ........................................ |
| Buildings insurance | £ ........................................ |
| Home contents insurance | £ ........................................ |
| Council tax | £ ........................................ |
| Maintenance/repairs | £ ........................................ |
| **Total housing costs** | £ ........................................ |

*Domestic costs:*

| | |
|---|---|
| Water rates | £ ........................................ |
| Gas | £ ........................................ |
| Electricity | £ ........................................ |
| Other fuel | £ ........................................ |
| Telephone | £ ........................................ |
| TV (licence/rental) | £ ........................................ |
| Other domestic costs | £ ........................................ |
| **Total domestic costs** | £ ........................................ |

*Housekeeping costs:*

| | |
|---|---|
| Food | £...................................... |
| Drink | £...................................... |
| Tobacco | £...................................... |
| Furnishings and equipment | £...................................... |
| Pets | £...................................... |
| Child care (part or full time) | £...................................... |
| Garden maintenance | £...................................... |
| Other housekeeping costs | £...................................... |
| **Total housekeeping costs** | **£......................................** |

*Transport costs:*

| | |
|---|---|
| Car repayments | £...................................... |
| Insurance | £...................................... |
| Tax | £...................................... |
| Maintenance/repair | £...................................... |
| Fuel | £...................................... |
| Recovery service (eg. AA/RAC) | £...................................... |
| Fares (buses/trains) | £...................................... |
| Other transport costs | £...................................... |
| **Total transport costs** | **£......................................** |

*Leisure costs:*

| | |
|---|---|
| Holidays | £...................................... |
| Entertainment (meals out etc.) | £...................................... |
| Club subscriptions (sports etc.) | £...................................... |
| Other leisure costs | £...................................... |
| **Total leisure costs** | **£......................................** |

*Personal costs:*

Clothing £........................................

Toiletries/cosmetics £........................................

Newspapers/magazines £........................................

Gifts £........................................

Books/music £........................................

Other personal costs £........................................

**Total personal costs** £........................................

*Financial costs:*

Life insurance £........................................

Travel insurance £........................................

Medical insurance £........................................

Other insurances £........................................

Credit card payments £........................................

Other card payments £........................................

Loan repayments £........................................

Hire purchase £........................................

School fees (cost/planning) £........................................

Pension contributions £........................................

Savings to bank/building society £........................................

Other savings £........................................

PEP investment £........................................

Other investments (shares etc.) £........................................

Tax/NI liabilities £........................................

Other financial costs £........................................

**Total financial costs** £........................................

Miscellaneous costs: £........................................

£........................................

£........................................

£........................................

**Total miscellaneous costs** £........................................

## TOTAL OUTGOINGS            £.........................................

Total income                 £.........................................
less
Total outgoings              £.........................................
equals
**FINAL BALANCE**            £.........................................

## ASSET PLANNER

Where the current value of an asset is not precisely known, as with a pension plan or endowment policy, use the current surrender value or transfer value (where applicable) in your calculations.

*Cash and cash equivalents:*

Bank savings account £......................................

Building society savings account £......................................

Other savings (TESSAs/cash etc.) £......................................

National Savings £......................................

**Total value of cash and cash equivalent** £......................................

*Investments:*

Life assurance plans with final value
(eg. endowments, bonds) £......................................

Personal equity plans £......................................

Unit trust investment £......................................

Investment trust investment £......................................

Stocks and shares £......................................

Overseas investment £......................................

**Total value of investments** £......................................

*Possessions:*

Main house/flat £......................................

Second home/holiday home £......................................

Other property £......................................

Car(s) £......................................

Boat(s) £......................................

Land £......................................

Antiques/paintings etc. £......................................

Jewellery £......................................

**Total value of possessions** £......................................

*Pension provisions:*
Personal pension plan £ ........................................
Company pension plan £ ........................................
Frozen pension plan assets £ ........................................
Other pension assets £ ........................................
**Total value of pension provisions** £ ..........................................

*Other assets:*
eg. money held in trust £ ........................................
£ ........................................
£ ........................................
£ ........................................
**Total value of other assets** £ ..........................................
**Total Assets** £ ..........................................

For your current net worth add up your liabilities using the list below and subtract them from your total assets.

*Liabilities:*

| | |
|---|---|
| Outstanding mortgage balance | £............................... |
| Bank overdraft | £............................... |
| Credit card balance | £............................... |
| Other outstanding loan balances | £............................... |
| Hire purchase balance | £............................... |
| Other liabilities | £............................... |
| Total value of liabilities | £............................... |
| **Total Liabilities** | £............................... |
| | |
| Total Assets | £............................... |
| less | |
| Total Liabilities | £............................... |
| equals | |
| **Current Net Worth** | £............................... |

◆

# Rushmere Wynne

are publishers of finance, investment and management books.
If you would like a copy of our current catalogue

*Please write to:*

Rushmere Wynne
4-5 Harmill
Grovebury Road
Leighton Buzzard
Bedfordshire
LU7 8FF

or Fax: 01525 852037

or Phone: 01525 853726